Functional Programming in PHP

Michael Bruno Lochemem

Functional Programming in PHP

A Primer for Composing Software in PHP

Apress®

Michael Bruno Lochemem
Nairobi, Kenya

ISBN 979-8-8688-2467-8   ISBN 979-8-8688-2468-5   (eBook)
https://doi.org/10.1007/979-8-8688-2468-5

Acknowledgements I would like to begin this list of acknowledgments by recognizing the efforts of the Apress team that facilitated the completion of this book. At the time of discovery by Divya Modi, the original work, which was published on Leanpub, though coherent, was in need of improvement. In providing an avenue to improve the material, Divya made it possible for me to work with Shobana Srinivasan and Gryffin Winkler, two editors who provided immense assistance during the writing process.

Next, I would like to thank my supervisor, Prof. Patrick Wamuyu; my mentor, Paul Bombo; my boss, Geert van Bommel; and my colleagues at MG Lotus Ltd— Dylan, Jesse, Harro, Wouter, Manon, and Davor—for inspiring confidence in me to embark on a rigorous writing journey.

Finally, I would like to extend my sincere, profuse thanks to my family for their unwavering support. To my parents, Bernadette Ocaya and the deceased Prof. Bruno Ocaya, I am forever grateful for all that you have done to nurture my interests in software engineering. From purchasing my first computer to paying for my education, the feats of your parenting have conditioned me to write this book I believe will prove helpful to those who read it. To my sisters, Frances, Consolate, and Faith, thank you for catalyzing writing efforts and, in particular, for spurring me on when I needed a boost.

Contents

About the Author

Michael Bruno Lochemem an alum of the United States International University-Africa and a current MG Lotus employee, is a software engineer and technical writer from Kampala, Uganda. Michael is a Functional Programming advocate and an avid promoter of Systems Programming and evented I/O. He is proficient in PHP, C, and JavaScript and actively maintains open source software that aligns closely with his technical interests. His portfolio of open source contributions includes PHP libraries like bingo-functional and asyncify and language extensions like ext-mrloop, ext-trie, and ext-picohttpparser.

Michael likes to publish articles that topically align with his interests on his blog hosted on Medium. He is a fan of the Miami Heat, Miami Dolphins, and FC Bayern Munich and plays basketball when he is not sitting at his desk.

About the Technical Reviewer

Sri Manikanta Palakollu is an accomplished software developer with five years of distinguished experience. He has demonstrated exceptional expertise across a diverse range of cutting-edge technologies, including Java, AEM, Python, Spring, Microservices, C++, C, JavaScript, TypeScript, MERN, databases, AI, and System Design.

Beyond his exceptional technical capabilities, Sri Manikanta is also a prolific and acclaimed writer. He has authored numerous insightful articles on influential topics such as artificial intelligence, machine learning, programming, data science, and cybersecurity. His work has been featured on prestigious platforms, including Medium, HackerNoon, and Analytics Vidhya. Furthermore, Sri Manikanta has contributed his technical expertise to several esteemed publications from renowned publishers such as Packt and Apress, including his own authored book, *Practical System Programming with C*.

In addition to his distinguished writing accomplishments, Sri Manikanta has showcased his expertise and creativity by winning a prestigious national-level hackathon. He also maintains an active involvement in numerous open source projects, demonstrating his passion for innovation and problem-solving. As a committed mentor, Sri Manikanta has guided over 5,000 students through coding hackathons organized by both national and international institutions and organizations.

Introduction

Functional Programming has long been a staple of modern computing. Since the advent of Lisp in 1960, on the premise of achieving machine intelligence via a computationally idiomatic encoding of the Lambda Calculus, the paradigm has undergone a non-monotonic evolution. Initially a darling of the mainstream, the paradigm has been forced outside its confines into the world of academia and has recently re-emerged in the zeitgeist as a wholesome approach to writing computer programs. What makes Functional Programming especially compelling is its emphasis on solving problems via composition, a process defined by the ability to parameterize aspects of answers and combine the functions created on parameterization.

The average PHP developer is likely to have encountered Functional Programming to the extent of deliberately or otherwise writing pure functions, applying some variation of composition, or invoking some nuanced paradigmatic technique. This book, targeted at professionals and hobbyists with intermediate- to advanced-level proficiency in PHP interested in Functional Programming, is a distillation of essential paradigmatic concepts that satiates the curiosity of those in the aforementioned skill categories, who, whether knowingly or not, might have dabbled in some Functional Programming before or are at least aware of its existence, but, more importantly, intrigued by its viability in PHP. It provides a ground-up instruction in expressing PHP programs as function composites by discussing the rudiments of Functional Programming, pure functions, immutability, and composition, before expositing more advanced paradigmatic patterns such as currying, functors, and Communicating Sequential Processes (CSP).

In reading this book, you will likely discover certain things about Functional Programming, as interspersed in its contents are refutations of falsehoods about the paradigm, descriptions of the origins of commonplace programming concepts that accurately portray it as a wellspring of popularized knowledge, and digestible breakdowns of paradigmatic jargon and techniques that might seem difficult to comprehend. It is my hope that you find the material you are about to peruse edifying and can, upon completion, espouse the Dao of Functional Programming—composition.

Chapter 1
An Introduction to Functional Programming

1.1 Defining Functional Programming

The process of software development is typified by the practice of breaking down larger problems into smaller ones. The result of this approach is often the creation of a solution—an application—by stitching together encodings of ideas that, in isolation, solve one of either a single problem or a subset of problems. Stitching together is, in this case, synonymous with defining rules, representing those rules in isolated, callable units, and applying those rules. Rules are explicit statements of intent. They are a means by which to define a task to complete and nothing more. Herein lies the definition of Functional Programming.

Functional Programming is an approach to building applications that is centered around composing pure functions (enforcements of rules) unburdened by the vagueness of side effects and side causes. Side effects and side causes are (ever-present) vectors that can, if unconstrained, invalidate rules and thence render functions impure. More on this later.

In drafting rules, writing, and subsequently invoking the functions that enforce their boundaries, the principle of abstraction takes center stage. Functions abstract rules, but more specifically, the actions undertaken to effect them: they tidy away rule-specific actions that are typically combinations of effectful expressions. Consider the problem of adding two integers. The rule, computing the sum of two integers, can be abstracted into the signature of an arbitrarily named function that takes two arguments as in the example to follow.

M. B. Lochemem, *Functional Programming in PHP*, https://doi.org/10.1007/979-8-8688-2468-5_1

A simple function to compute the sum of two numbers

```
function add(int $x, int $y): int
{
  return $x + $y;
}

echo add(1, 7);
```

The function "add" contains the semantics of the desired summation—a simple expression that effects the sum of two operands, the two arguments named "x" and "y." Beyond the rule and its implementation, the invocation of the "add" function represents the rule in effect. The expectation is such that the sum of 1 and 7, as computed by "add," yields 8 and will do so every time the arguments are 1 and 7. Because there are no vectors that could change the "add" function's behavior, the rule it is based on is never undermined, and thus, the function's purity is upheld. Such is the nature of Functional Programming.

> The Real World

Functions like those featured in the previous snippet are ideal and, sadly, fail to fully represent the real world where the rule-breaking vectors inherent to network and file Input/Output (I/O) feature prominently. They do, however, help communicate paradigmatic principles and the possible outcomes achievable with techniques yet to be discussed in future sections of the book.

1.2   Functional Programming Is Declarative and Imperative

Thus far, decent ground has been covered in regard to describing the declarative nature of Functional Programming. For a syntax to be considered declarative, it has to condition in its users a willingness to describe computations abstractly. In Functional Programming, this abstractness manifests not only in the tidying away of operations but also in the mental real estate of the programmer, as a pronounced focus on the intent defined in rules. No artifact embodies the ideals of declarative programming better than expressions. Expressions are effectful statements through which to apply rules. They often consist of some combination of function calls and operations with one or several operands and are yet another fixture in day-to-day programming.

An assortment of valid expressions in PHP

```
2 * 2;

\array_filter(
  \range(1, 5),
  fn (int $x): bool => $x % 2 === 0,
);

'foo' . '-bar';

\SplFixedArray::fromArray(
  [
    'foo',
    'bar',
    'qux',
  ],
);
```

The results of expressions like those shown in the snippet above can be stored in memory in such a way as to render them reusable throughout an accessible scope of an application—via an assignment operation. In fact, this is another practice that is commonplace in everyday programming—particularly of the procedural kind. With procedural programming, every result is holstered in memory for often near-immediate or sometimes future use. Consider the snippet below.

A program that demonstrates a procedural approach to adding numbers

```
$x = 1 + 7;
$y = $x + 3;
$z = $y + 2;

echo $z;
```

There are, in the example, three successive addition expressions that each effect the addition rule that informed the creation of the "add" function from the previous segment. Each result, bar the last, is used in a subsequent expression, and every binding holsters itself in the programmer's mental real estate. With calls to a pure function like the one from the previous segment, the successive bindings can effectively be reduced to a single one. In exploring this, it is possible to chain rules and, thus, the functions that enforce them—as in the modifications below.

A demonstration of the replacement of imperative addition with function application

```
$z = add(
  add(
    add(1, 7), // $x
    3, // $y
  ),
  2, // $z
);

echo $z;
```

The three bindings from earlier do not exist in the snippet above. They have effectively been replaced with a composition of calls to the pure "add" function. The replacement does not alter the imperative nature of the program but rather refines it with composition. Function chains in which the output of one call to a pure function is propagated as the input of the one that follows it reduce the likelihood of the impurities (vectors) in certain expressions compounding over sequenced assignments. It is, therefore, safe to assert that Functional Programming conditions its practitioners to engage in "safe," vector-controlled, rule-respecting imperative-style development.

1.3 History of Functional Programming

The roots of Functional Programming are traceable to the seminal works of Alonzo Church and Alan Turing. Church advanced the Lambda Calculus, a mathematical notation that emphasizes using functions as rules for turning inputs into outputs (more on this later), in the 1930s. His doctoral student, Turing, shortly after, put forward the idea of a Universal Machine, an emulation of a device capable of making axiomatic computations—one capable of solving problems in discrete steps (algorithms). While Church's Lambda Calculus provided a syntax for the abstraction that characterizes Functional Programming, Turing's hypothesis laid out the fundamental means of designing and executing computer programs.

Almost two decades after the inception of the Lambda Calculus and Universal Turing Machine emerged the first real Functional Programming language—Lisp. The world into which Lisp was introduced was one primed for modern computing. By the time Lisp was first released for the IBM 704 in 1958, the transistor and von Neumann stored-program concept had already taken a foothold in computing. By creating Lisp, John McCarthy realized a syntax that resembles the notation in Church's Lambda Calculus and adheres to the computation-by-algorithm rubric in Turing's Universal Machine. McCarthy's work on Lisp also pioneered ideas such as dynamic binding, garbage collection, recursion, and higher-order functions—

ideas that characterize the complexion of modern computer programming today. In offshoots like Scheme, Clojure, Janet, and Phel (more on this later), Lisp lives on to this day.

In the 1970s, Functional Programming, and, in particular, the Lisp variants of that time, began to cede popularity to object-oriented and procedural strategies. Smalltalk, one of two major competitors in that decade, was created in 1972 in Palo Alto. With its inception came an ideology centered around using objects and the methods defined in them to shuttle data in applications. The ideals of Alan Kay, the then leader of the Xerox Palo Alto Research Center (PARC) team that created Smalltalk, were, in reality, not completely divorced from those of Church and Turing, but nevertheless established the foundations of Object-Oriented Programming as we know it today.

C, the other major competitor, was conceived in 1978 after two failures—Multics and the B programming language. The former was an attempt at creating an Operating System (OS) that was ultimately derailed by its lead engineers—Dennis Ritchie and Ken Thompson—failing to optimize its kernel for the hardware it was intended to run on. The latter, a creation of Thompson's, was characterized by a suboptimal compiler and an incomplete type system. The version of C that became a mainstay in computer programming overcame the challenges in the projects that directly preceded it and offered a mostly imperative approach to building computer programs.

The creation of Haskell in the late 1980s by a team of academics did little to stem the momentous tide of alternative programming approaches, as the paradigm was pushed further to the periphery of mainstream programming in the decades that ensued. The recent revival of Functional Programming began around the time paradigm constructs started to feature prominently in large codebases of popular software. Around the 2010s, the first real hints of a revival came in the form of Twitter shipping Scala and Clojure rewrites of their backend code. Scala and Clojure were, at the time, fairly new additions to the Java Virtual Machine (JVM) and offered some real upside for the company's scaling efforts despite having small communities at the moment of first adoption. Twitter's adoption of Functional Programming tooling was soon followed by Facebook's back-to-back rollouts of Flow, an OCaml-powered type checker for JavaScript, and Haxl, a spam filter written in Haskell, in 2014 and 2015, respectively. The goodwill earned through the successes of these endeavors prompted industry-wide reacceptance of Functional Programming ideas and, thus, a re-entry of those ideas into the mainstream.

1.4 Functional Programming and PHP

PHP was developed in 1995 at a time when Functional Programming occupied the ideological territory on the periphery of mainstream computer programming. Perl was the darling of scripting languages during this period and was one of many key influences on the earliest designs of the PHP language. Baked into early

PHP were Perl's dollar-sign-prefixed variables, regular expressions, and Common Gateway Interface (CGI) bindings. It is worth noting that these features are still fixtures of modern PHP. The language, in its infancy, was a neat wrapper around Perl and C whose purpose was simplifying web page content rendering while simultaneously providing a small performance benefit. Compounding functions into full-on applications in PHP's earliest versions was a strenuous task as every function, except those provided out of the box, had to be written in C, added to a symbol table, registered as a grammatical tool in a parser-generator file, and compiled so as to be operationalized for calls in the language userspace. Working Functional Programming patterns like the ones you will see later in this book into projects written in PHP I, or its successor, PHP/FI (Form Interpreter), was discernably difficult when PHP was freshly incepted: after all, the language was, at this stage, almost exclusively useful for small projects.

In reaching out to Rasmus Lerdorf in the late 1990s via mailing list to discuss improvements to the PHP/FI project, Zeev Suraski and Andi Gutmans began the work of rewriting the PHP interpreter to offer more out-of-the-box userspace features. First worked into PHP 3 and then refined in PHP 4, the Zend engine, effectively the revamped interpreter created by the two Israeli programmers in consort with Mr. Lerdorf, ushered in artifacts that feature prominently in applications written in modern variants of the language. With the engine came a slate of artifacts like classes, namespaces, constants, and user-defined and anonymous functions that are all relevant to Functional Programming. In the early 2000s when PHP 4 was released, Object Orientation was the eminent paradigm. C++, Java, and C#, all multipurpose languages that exemplify the principles of Object-Oriented Programming, were ever-present across the realms of Systems Programming, web development, and desktop application development. Naturally, PHP took on and still retains a bend toward Object Orientation.

The versions of PHP that have followed the monumental fourth one have all shipped some combination of new functions, deprecations, and general engine performance improvements. The language artifacts well suited to the needs of Functional Programming have remained mostly intact through PHP's continued evolution. Functions have retained their first-class citizenry through most of the newer versions of PHP and, despite the ecosystem's pronounced emphasis on patterns centered around SOLID principles, have also mostly subtly retained their latent potential for use in Functional Programming. PHP, in its current state, complements its core of Functional Programming artifacts with interpreter enhancements, such as arrow functions, a match operator, and, soon, pipe syntax. At present, PHP is just as equipped to enable Functional Programming as any other programming language whose core fundamentals have been adapted to advance its ethos of encoding rules and composing the pure functions that best enforce their dictates.

1.5 Functional Programming Lightens Cognitive Load

It would be remiss to discuss Functional Programming's rationale and origins with little mention of the cognitive benefit that accrues to those who adopt its principles. Abstraction and rule-based composition lighten the strain on the working memory of programmers. Computer programming, like a lot of tasks that require one to attentively reason about concepts—solving a series of mathematical equations, writing a paper, and whatnot—has the capacity to overwhelm one's working memory. The limitation of working memory is such that its information space, referred to as the mental real estate earlier in this chapter, is only accommodative of about seven or so entries—quanta. This real estate gets new tenancy every 30 seconds or so and, thus, requires additional mental effort to retain information a little longer than its lifespan.

Composing pure functions helps programmers achieve valuable mental real estate savings. If each variable in a program can be thought of as occupying a quantum of information in the brain's working memory information space, programs written in such a way as to rely exclusively on the effects of each assignment put significant strain on the finite mental real estate of a programmer. Think back to the imperative sequential addition problem from earlier in the text. The summation results assigned to each variable $x, $y, and $z each registered an entry in working memory. In eliminating $x and $y via composition, albeit with a regular chain of function calls, the strain on working memory was somewhat alleviated: the slots reserved for $x and $y were vacated.

Functional Programming prescribes the expression of intent in as concise a manner as possible. While assignment is not a bad thing in and of itself, is generally unavoidable, and can be managed even under strenuous effect workloads, it is best reserved for operations that require a longer presence in an algorithm and, thus, a longer lifespan in working memory. The downstream effect of enforcing rules via functions that neatly tidy away effects, composed with terse assignments where necessary, is a lower Signal-to-Noise ratio. If the ability to create programs from well-formed artifacts that can fit well together and can be comprehended in isolation is a quality that best exemplifies the signal and the analog of the noise is a combination of all the stressors on the conciseness of a program, then composing functions in such a way as to encode all the useful rule rubric without introducing more artifact bindings than required produces a clearer signal.

This segment concludes the introductory chapter of the book. The next chapter will flesh out the fundamentals of the Functional Programming paradigm, expanding on the ideas of function purity, which was briefly discussed earlier, as well as referential transparency, the standard by which purity is measured, and immutability, a quality that defines the rigidity of the paradigm.

Chapter 2
Functional Programming Core Concepts

2.1 The Lambda Calculus

In the beginning, there was the Lambda Calculus. Alonzo Church devised, in the 1930s, a concise syntax for function application that would go on to formalize the fundamental ideas of the Functional Programming paradigm. The Lambda Calculus, like its offshoots, is a formal syntax complete with variables, expressions, and, most importantly, functions. It is a means of solving problems through a two-step function application process that starts with the substitution of arguments and ends in the evaluation of the expressions to which the arguments are applied. Imagine being asked to calculate the circumference of a circle with a radius of 5 units. Solving such a problem with the Lambda Calculus means creating a function that abstracts a suitable expression into which arbitrary arguments can be plugged with every invocation. A valid notational representation of a function with which to solve the circumference problem is as follows.

$$CIRCUMFERENCE = \lambda r[2\pi r] \tag{2.1}$$

The lambda (λ) in the notation above is the starting point of any encoding in the Lambda Calculus. It is instructive insofar as signaling the substitutability of all the variables that follow it: those local to the expression in the function and thence referred to as "bound." The λ effectively denotes a λ-term that signals that the expression that follows it—that in the square brackets—is ready to be applied to values assignable to all (local) "bound" variables when its host function is called. As far as the circumference encoding is concerned, the local variable is r, and the evaluable expression is $2\pi r$. In following through with the example, the computational steps shown below should yield a valid circumference.

$$(CIRCUMFERENCE)5 = (\lambda r[2\pi r])5 \triangleright 2 \times \pi \times 5 \tag{2.2}$$

M. B. Lochemem, *Functional Programming in PHP*,
https://doi.org/10.1007/979-8-8688-2468-5_2

$$= 10\pi \tag{2.3}$$

$$= approx.31.4159 \tag{2.4}$$

The calculation shown above is such that every occurrence of r is replaced with the value 5 before the arithmetic is effected, and the result is ultimately computed. The two-step function application process shown above is the β-conversion (or β-reduction), essentially the Golden Rule of the Lambda Calculus, and the gateway to function composition—as you will see later in the book. All computations in the Lambda Calculus, and, by extension, Functional Programming, are essentially abstractions of rules encoded as functions over relevant values per the principle of the β-conversion, the identity for which appears below.

$$(\lambda x[M])N \triangleright M[x := N] \tag{2.5}$$

Given an expression M, a variable x, and an argument N, all occurrences of x in the expression M need be swapped with the value assignable to N. Such is the interpretation of the β-conversion. Because of this rule orientation, the Lambda Calculus allows for distinct forms of otherwise equivalent functions to exist. What this means is that notationally, functions that are semantically different but implement the same rule are considered distinct—like synonyms in the English language. If the circumference function from before were to be rewritten as in the snippet below, the resultant function, and, thence, the resultant substitution on application, would more or less produce the same result, but retain distinguishability.

$$(CIRCUMFERENCE)5 = (\lambda r[\pi r + \pi r])5 \triangleright \pi \times 5 + \pi \times 5 \tag{2.6}$$

$$= approx.31.4159 \tag{2.7}$$

The principle shown above is known as **hyperintensionality**. Hyperintensionality implies that multiple variants of a rule, each with a subtle, distinctive quality, are permissible. In practice, the slight contextual differences between functions designed to implement the same rule often prove consequential. Imagine two variants of a JSON decoder—one that implements a linear parser and another that relies on Single Instruction, Multiple Data (SIMD) parsing routines. The latter is temporally more efficient than the former, but nevertheless converts a JSON string to a hashtable. Now that it is clear how functions are created and used in the Lambda Calculus, the next step is to evaluate the varieties of functions available in PHP and the modalities of function use in the language.

2.2 Functions in PHP

Functions are, as emphasized thus far, implementations of rules. Rules are, per the Lambda Calculus, relationships between inputs and outputs, and therefore, functions are too, in a transitive way. Functions have no histories, and for this reason, they are generally cheaper in terms of working memory real estate than other artifacts that are generally more prone to change. In PHP, functions are first-class citizens. They are definable and thence usable in a variety of expression contexts and data structures. Anatomically, functions have a mostly universal structure that consists of a keyword, a parenthesized parameter list, and a signature for localized expressions. When a function is invoked with arguments, each value assigned to each argument is substituted for every occurrence of the corresponding argument in its signature, as in the Lambda Calculus: the β-conversion holds in PHP.

A named function with which to compute the difference between two numbers

```
function subtract(int $x, int $y): int
{
    return $x - $y;
}

echo subtract(6, 3);
```

The named (or user-defined) function `subtract` shown in the snippet above is an example of perhaps the most common variant of function in PHP. Already featured in the text, the named function is a mainstay in language codebases that have a bend toward Functional Programming. Such functions can be namespaced, loaded conditionally when placed in the scope of a control artifact like an if-statement, called recursively, and encoded for future reference as either a string or a first-class callable—as of PHP 8.1. Named functions, for all their ubiquity and intuitiveness, require manual loading when placed in separate files, however. Regardless, they offer a high degree of versatility, especially in projects characterized by rich namespace topologies.

The next type of function in the PHP userspace is the anonymous function. Named so because of the distinctive lack of an explicit function name upon definition, the anonymous function (or lambda) is often either assigned to a variable, placed inside another data structure capable of accommodating it, shuttled as a function parameter, or tuned in such a way as to provide a suitable return value. Anonymous functions are usable in a vast variety of scopes—global and otherwise—and generally retain all of the semantic features of user-defined functions except for the explicit name.

An anonymous function with which to concatenate two strings

```php
$concat = function (string $x, string $y): string {
  return $x . $y;
};

echo $concat('Hello, ', 'World');
```

Anonymous functions, when defined in such a way as to access scopes outside of their signatures—external jurisdictions with foreign states—are regarded as closures. The aforedescribed closure behavior is not built into anonymous functions by default in PHP, unlike in Common Lisp or JavaScript, but is rather a feature whose activation is left to the discretion of the programmer. By passing a parenthesized list of variables of interest that reside in a foreign scope via the use keyword, it is possible to create a closure, or a lambda as it is known in other more explicitly functional languages.

A closure with which to divide a dividend by a foreign divisor

```php
$divisor = 4;

$divide = fn (float $dividend) use ($divisor): float {
  return $dividend / $divisor;
};

echo $divide(12);
```

Using closures in PHP as in the example above, to access the divisor ultimately means trading the compactness of a lean function anatomy for more conciseness and, with it, more verboseness in determining the data that is admitted into the lambda signature. While the verboseness associated with the use keyword allows for specificity, it might not be the best fit for situations that require a lean function expression. The arrow function, the most recently added variant of anonymous function, is well suited to such situations. Arrow functions have signatures that can only accommodate a single return expression—a limitation that can, in the right context, be overcome with carefully applied composition. To follow is an elegant rewrite of the previous division operation, a one-liner that almost replicates the conciseness of the circumference function in the Lambda Calculus primer.

An arrow function with which to compute a quotient from the division of a dividend by a foreign divisor

```php
$divisor = 4;

$divide = fn (float $dividend): float => $dividend / $divisor;

echo $divide(12);
```

The last type of function, but certainly not the least, is the class method, or simply the method. Classes and objects are staples of the PHP programming experience, and so are the functions defined in them. Such artifacts have immense value, despite most of the examples in the text thus far centering on named functions. Methods are bound by the conventional rules of class artifact visibility and scope access and are especially useful when defined in classes in such a way as to offer a means of modifying the properties that exist alongside them without inducing any rule-breaking vectors.

A simple Operations class with a method that computes the sum of the numbers passed to its constructor

```php
class Operations
{
  public function __construct(
    private int $x,
    private int $y,
  ) {
  }

  public function add(): int
  {
    return $this->x + $this->y;
  }
}

var_dump(
  (new Operations(1, 2))
    ->add(),
);
```

The simple class shown above has two methods—a constructor through which to create a new object and thence operationalize the class with two integer inputs and an add method that effects the sum of the two properties in a given instance of the class. As far as classes are concerned, the more intact their properties can remain in a single instance, the purer the objects spawned from them. This is important to remember as classes present a slightly nuanced proposition in Functional Programming.

> **Autoloading PHP Functions**

Autoloading is one of PHP's defining features. It optimizes the everyday practice of loading project-relevant artifacts into the scripts where they are needed, seeing as it is commonplace for PHP developers to write code in such a way as to place one or a small number of related artifacts in a single script file. Autoloading is a catch-all mechanism such that artifacts whose names are synonymous with the files in which their contents reside are automatically loaded into the entry point of an application—its autoloader. The practice of loading artifacts via an autoloader preemptively declutters the header sections of PHP scripts that, in non-autoloading schemes, would feature several include directives.

For all the joys of not having to go through what in large projects would otherwise be a laundry list of includes, there is a downside to autoloading in its present constitution: it applies most readily, and almost exclusively, to classes, interfaces, traits, and enumerations. Herein lies a problem. User-defined functions, already highlighted as definable in the same way as the aforelisted object-oriented artifacts—in a one instance per file scheme—cannot be readily included via the same core autoloading utilities. While there have been ameliorative RFCs tabled for consideration, the best solution for function autoloading is using the Composer autoloader, which is essentially a static hashtable with loadable paths. By defining a list of paths to files that each contain a user-defined function in the files segment of a project's composer.json file, it is possible to register relevant functions and effectively operationalize the autoloader to condition behavior typical of class autoloading. Please keep this in mind moving forward.

2.2.1 *Functional Programming and Object Orientation*

The original premise of Object Orientation was efficient message passing. Alan Kay, the creator of the paradigm, sought to actualize a version of data interchange modeled after the behavior of biological cells. In the pursuit of his vision, Kay implemented an enhanced version of the "big object"—a metastructure containing pointers to both data and functions—and, in so doing, created an artifact capable of hiding localized state modifications. While developing the shell of the "big object," Kay researched lambda expressions in Lisp and worked them into his model upon concluding that they were pivotal for abstracting the arbitrary rules that would govern localized state processing. He also worked in Lisp's runtime (or late) data binding to ensure that functions defined on objects could be modified in a discretionary way without cajoling a compiler.

A favorable interpretation of Kay's work on Smalltalk, the foundational syntax into which he ultimately incorporated his ideas, is that objects are media for data interchange that enforce the original ideas of the Lambda Calculus. The original Object Orientation manifesto prioritizes the use of artifacts with hidden states, the transformations of which are abstracted into special algebras (functions) that are also native to them. As such, using objects warrants a consideration of purity that extends beyond the methods defined on them. To use objects in fulfillment of Kay's manifesto, special attention should be given to the makeup of encapsulated states and the changes that can be rendered onto them by the methods with which they co-exist.

2.3 Pure Functions

For a function to be considered pure, it has to uphold the rule it implements for every possible combination of inputs it receives. The idea of function purity is similar to the concept of a contract, wherein a function is a contractor that is only considered effective and thus operating within the limits of a binding agreement when acting in such a way as to fulfill stipulated objectives without breaching stipulated terms. Purity is easy to enforce in scenarios like those in Chap. 1, where the problems do not require interactions with outside entities—filesystems, databases, third-party APIs, and such. In such contexts, it is easy to identify artifacts capable of inducing rule-breaking behavior, like global variables that are prone to change. Consider the example to follow.

A simple program that features a function rendered impure by a mutable global variable

```php
$acc = 0;

function add(int $x, int $y): int
{
   global $acc;

   return $acc + $x + $y;
}

$acc += 2;

echo add(2, 3) . PHP_EOL;
```

The **add** function featured in the snippet is similar to that from Chap. 1. To internalize the concept of impurity, it helps to imagine the function as extant in a context where addition is reliant on some accumulator—much like a calculator. Now, a default accumulator value of zero ensures that the addition function always produces the pure sum of two integers. If, for some reason, the accumulator is haphazardly modified between calls to the **add** function, the summation rule ceases to be valid. Instead of outputting 5, the sum of the integers 2 and 3, the function, but more specifically the parameterized expression inside of it, evaluates to 7 to reflect the change in the global accumulator. Conceptually, the threat of a modification to a global variable, as in the example, would constitute a hypothetical side cause, and the result of the haphazard modification would be considered a side effect. Such are the rule-breaking vectors to look out for when attempting to write pure functions.

2.3.1 Side Causes and Side Effects

Practically, it is impossible to avoid impurities. When discussing rule-breaking, it is imperative to consider potential behavior-altering threats, as well as any unaccounted-for modifications to program state that those threats, if unmitigated, can inflict. A side cause, per this line of thought, is a threat capable of triggering a side effect—a consequence of an unhandled threat. Identifying rule-breaking vectors in everyday programming is complicated not just by the number of subsystems the typical production application interacts with, but also by the implications of the various modalities of data interchange. A deletion operation in a remote database can set off a cascade of deletions in an application that relies on it; a thread could potentially rewrite critical parts of a shared application state. Such potential realities have implications for function design.

Seeing as impurity has a cause-and-effect feel to it, functions should generally be written in anticipation of vectors capable of invalidating rules and, worse still, unintentionally changing the makeup of the state into which they are applicable. To this end, the following shortlist of regularly occurring impurities should provide some insight into what to fortify functions against:

1. **Mutable global variables**, like the accumulator in the most recent example.
2. **Input/Output (I/O)** of the network and disk varieties. This categorization includes changes that can be brought about by database queries, network requests, and file reads and writes.
3. **Exceptions** that halt the runtime when encountered and bring programs to a standstill, thereby preventing further attempts at composition.
4. **Functions with generally inconsistent return values** that do not return the same outputs given the same inputs, like `time()` and `rand()`.

The remedies for the aforelisted side causes, and thus the side effects they are associated with, are, depending on how complex the problem they are designed to feature in is, either as simple as using closures or as rigorous as using any one or a combination of the specialized data structures and conventions discussed later in the book.

2.3.2   Referential Transparency

Pure functions are referentially transparent. They exhibit behavior such that every invocation with a particular set of arguments is substitutable with its result. The sum of 4 and 3 is 7; swapping 7 with an invocation of the add function from earlier with the arguments 4 and 3 demonstrates this substitutability. Intuitively, the question to ask when trying to ascertain whether a function is referentially transparent or not is: "Can I replace a call to the function, with certain arguments, with the result of the parameterized function call?" Referential transparency conditions those familiar with it to think of functions as black boxes—tiny expression engines with opaque internals but known inputs and outputs. Such thinking presents certain advantages.

The first significant benefit of referential transparency is its ability to operationalize the hyperintensionality of Functional Programming. By thinking purely in terms of inputs and outputs, it is possible to roll different, contextually fitting versions of certain functions into expressions without breaking any adjacent program states. If there were to arise a need to harden a secure message passing system because of a decision to adopt a stronger cryptographic algorithm, for instance, swapping minimally viable cryptography for more hardened security without changing any of the keys required for encipherment and decipherment would certainly satisfy the rules of expression distinctness and the preconditions for referential transparency. Black-box thinking would, in this hypothetical case, set the targets of a useful implementation and require of the programmer optimal expressions—the contents of the black box.

Testing code is yet another everyday practice in software development. In writing tests, proofs that a program performs as it should, assertions—declarations of behavior-defining conditions—are rendered subject to evaluation. The behavior of artifacts written in such a way as to be easily reasoned about, like pure functions, is easy to form declarations about and thus evaluate on the merits of function inputs and outputs. Another benefit of referential transparency is its ability to guide the formulation of testable assertions. If one were to test the accuracy of the add function from earlier, as in the snippet to follow, emphasis would be placed on proving, via an assertion engine, that any two integer inputs and their sum are substitutable.

A simple assertion with which to affirm the referential transparency of a pure function that computes the sum of two numbers

```
class AddTest
{
  public function testaddComputesTheSumOfTwoNumbers(): void
  {
    $this->assertEquals(
      7,
      sum(3, 4),
    );
  }
}
```

The assertion above would pass in perpetuity if the version of the add function tested is the one that does not depend on a modifiable, and ultimately modified, global accumulator. In sharpening assertions made about functions based on their inputs and outputs, referential transparency, by extension, renders unnecessary assignments and repetitive expressions replaceable via composition. Think back to Chap. 1 in which each assignment in a multi-step addition sequence was replaced by a function call to a pure function, the parameters and result of which were known. Below is a refresher.

Referential Transparency as a vehicle for composition and precise assignment operations

```
$z = add(
  add(
    add(1, 7),   // $x = 1 + 7;
    3,           // $y = $x + 3;
  ),
  2,             // $z = $y + 2;
);

echo $z;
```

In swapping each assignment for a function call, the needless duplication of the addition expression in multiple assignments is reduced to a single plug-and-use parameterized expression. While assignment is not to be avoided, it is best used sparingly as a means of increasing the potential for reuse of variables. For this reason, referential transparency also conditions the use of variables according to rules that underpin the use of pure functions. Intuitively, this can be understood as an approach to expression building in which an artifact—such as a variable, function, or object—is declared once and reused whenever there is a need to swap certain workable inputs for a deterministic result.

2.3.2.1 Type Signatures

Referential transparency's black-box approach to describing functions solely in terms of what they can process and the outputs they ultimately produce can be represented in a precise complementary notation referred to as a type (or function) signature. A type signature is a succinct, annotative description of the data categories of a function's inputs and outputs. Each type signature has the expressive power to communicate, in a terse meta language, the intent of a function. Type signatures are significant in Functional Programming so much that they are woven into the compilers of typed functional languages like Haskell and OCaml as *pseudo*-static analyzers and inference engines. In PHP, they are mostly consigned to comment blocks and have no real use outside of enhancing the documentation of pure functions.

Type signatures are generally written in the Hindley–Milner style, in a syntax that generally accommodates strict and polymorphic types. Strict type definitions are rather straightforward in that they feature absolute, concrete data categories. Such annotations are associated with functions for which the parameters and outputs are of a (mostly) single, readily discernible type in the language userspace, like an integer, object, boolean, or string. Consider the examples below.

Functions and their respective Hindley-Milner type signatures

```
// add :: Int -> Int -> Int
function add(int $x, int $y): int
{
  return $x + $y;
}

// slugify :: Array -> String
function slugify(array $inputs): string
{
  return \implode('-', $inputs);
}

// divide :: Int -> Int -> (Object -> Int) -> Int
function divide(
  int $dividend,
  int $divisor,
  callable $error,
): int {
  try {
    return \intdiv($dividend, $divisor);
  } catch (Throwable $err) {
    return (int) $error($err);
  }
}
```

In the annotation of the first function, two integer inputs are required to generate an integer output. In the annotation of the second, a string is generated from an array, and finally, in that of the third, two integers and a lambda—the expression enclosed in parentheses—are the arguments of a function that produces an integer. Each of the featured signatures showcases concrete primitives native to the PHP type system.

Polymorphic types, unlike their strict counterparts, are not explicit but denote categories whose runtime relevance can be inferred by the reader. A polymorphic type is often represented as a single, arbitrarily named variable, typically a single letter or two, that cannot be conflated with a canonical userspace type, like those featured in the most recent example. The examples to follow should prove demonstrative.

Type signatures with polymorphic types

```
// id :: a -> a
function id(mixed $value): mixed
{
  return $value;
}

// head :: [a] -> a
function head(array $list): mixed
{
  \reset($list);

  return \current($list);
}
```

The first function in the snippet above is the identity function—one that returns the value passed to it. Its annotation suggests that any value, of any type, when passed, will be returned. The variable that denotes the argument type a is the same as that which indicates the return type, as the input and output are the same for the identity function.

The annotation for head, the second function in the example, is a little more interesting. Without examining the function signature, it is correct to infer that its annotation suggests that it takes an array containing elements of a certain type, a, and transforms that list into a single value of the same type. Such a type signature does not indicate the specific array element that the function that implements it returns. It is therefore polymorphic as it works for any one of the entries in a hypothetical array of the runtime-assignable type, a. Only when accounting for the expressions in the signature of the head function does it become clear that it retrieves the first entry in a list passed to it.

Fluency in writing type signatures implies a writer's ability to clearly express intent that a reader can parse to infer the possible inner workings of annotated functions. Future chapters of the book feature type signatures with sum types and contexts, signatures that situationally enhance the ideas discussed in this segment, which can be considered a primer on effectively encoding referential transparency.

2.4 Immutability

Designing for referential transparency means designing for reusability. Reusable artifacts have an unchanging nature and are unlikely to induce side effects as a result. While it is generally desirable to use functions for everything as they seldom change, leave no historical footprint, and can be invoked as many times as required, they do not always offer the best means of persisting constant expressions. Artifacts like constants and persistent data structures provide not only the syntactic rigor that functions are not always guaranteed to provide when dealing with such expressions, but also a promise of a peaceful co-existence alongside pure functions whose rules are not to be violated.

2.4.1   Constants

A constant is a placeholder for a value that can neither be modified nor redeclared during the execution of a program. Constants are some of the only case-sensitive artifacts in the PHP userspace and are mostly written in uppercase characters with underscore separators interspersed where necessary. There are two ways to declare constants in PHP. The first approach relies on the use of the `const` keyword, and the second requires a call to the `define` function.

Defining constants in PHP

```
const MULTIPLIER = 12;

\define('DECIMAL_BASE_RANGE', \range(0, 9));
```

Constants defined via the `const` keyword can only be assigned expressions whose operands are scalar values. Only strings, integers, floating-point numbers, boolean values, and arrays containing the aforelisted types are workable. Such constants can be namespaced, like functions, and can be used in much the same way, but must be declared in a top-level scope that is neither a function, loop, `if`-statement, nor `try/catch` block.

Defining constants via the const keyword

```
namespace Acme;

// bitwise OR operation with JSON constants (constant expression)
const JSON_ENCODE_OPTIONS = JSON_PRETTY_PRINT |
JSON_ENCODE_ZERO_FRACTION;

// string template
const MESSAGE_FORMAT = "Hello, %s";

// sin(360)
const SIN_360 = 0.9589;
```

The `define` function has none of the limitations associated with the const keyword. The constants defined by calling it can be assigned several kinds of expressions not limited to scalar values and arrays that contain them. Furthermore, such constants do not have the same scope restrictions and can be used in both top-level and more specialized scopes.

Defining constants via the define function

```php
namespace Acme;

\define(
  'ADD_CHECK',
  // function check
  \function_exists(__NAMESPACE__ . '\\add'),
);

function add(int $x, int $y): int
{
  // scoped to function
  \define('acc', 0);

  return acc + $x + $y;
}

$list = [22, 31];

if (ADD_CHECK) {
  var_dump(
    add(...$list),
  );
}
```

PHP also allows for the definition of constants in classes. Such constants behave like those that can be created via the `const` keyword and are, like methods, also subject to the rules of artifact visibility. Accessing such artifacts requires a scope resolution operator (`::`), a syntactic element synonymous with static methods.

Defining constants in PHP classes

```php
class Calculator
{
  private const ACCUMULATOR = 0;

  public const COS_90 = -0.4481;

  public function add(int $x, int $y): int
  {
```

```
    return self::ACCUMULATOR + $x + $y;
  }
}

var_dump(
  (new Calculator())->add(2, 3),
  Calculator::COS_90,
);
```

It helps to think of the values assigned to constants as reusable, either as templates for eventual modification via a function call or as operands that can be directly plugged into expressions. Constant expressions, because of their unchangeability, reduce the likelihood of haphazard modifications occurring. When accounting for the versatility of **define** and strictness of **const**, the applicability of constants is commensurate with the size of the problem space from which constant expressions can be formed.

2.4.2   *Persistent Data Structures*

Constants, though mightily useful, are not effective when there arises a need to manage artifact histories. Structures built to preserve all (usable) versions of trackable data while avoiding the penalties of haphazard external state modification are certainly worth considering. Persistent data structures, as their name suggests, allow for such preservation. Such structures are, in PHP, mostly creatable from classes whose design dictates that each spawnable object encapsulates one state and one state only. Persistent objects propagate different versions of themselves with each function call. To demonstrate object purity via persistent data structure, a simple `Calculator` class with an internal accumulator should suffice.

A Calculator class that is a template for a persistent data structure

```
class Calculator
{
  public function __construct(
    private int $acc = 0,
  ) {
  }

  public function multiply(int $x): self
  {
    return new static($this->acc * $x);
  }

  public function subtract(int $x): self
```

```php
  {
    return new static($this->acc - $x);
  }

  public function value(): int
  {
    return $this->acc;
  }
}

$result = (new Calculator())
  ->subtract(2)                 // = 0 - 2
  ->multiply(4)                 // = -2 * 4
  ->value();                    // = -8

echo $result;
```

The design of the class featured above is such that the value of the encapsulated accumulator can only be updated via successive method calls. Each time either the `subtract` or `multiply` method is called, the accumulator is assigned a new value, but in a new object. Each accumulator version is retained in a predecessor object from which a new chain can be started altogether. Although chains like that featured above can theoretically (though impractically) continue in perpetuity, they provide a means of keeping all accumulator versions in some kind of *pseudo*linked list. Whenever classes, and by extension the objects that can be spawned from them, are created in such a way as to favor forward chaining via successive method calls that each reflexively create a fresh one-of-a-kind instance, they are generally considered persistent. Immutable lists and tries are two persistent structures that bring the aforedescribed linked-list-like feel to PHP.

2.4.2.1 Immutable Lists

Immutable lists are simply persistent array structures. Every such list is an object whose primary state constituent is an array, the versions of which can be tracked through a series of specific modificatory function calls. In PHP, immutable lists can be created from userland implementations in packages like phunkie and immutable-php. The example below, however, utilizes the version of the structure in the bingo-functional library that is powered by the ds extension's vector and, when absent, the SPL fixed array.

Instantiating and using an immutable list in PHP

```php
use Chemem\Bingo\Functional\Immutable\Collection;

// initialize token list
```

```
$tokens = Collection::from(
  [
    'functional',
    'programming',
    'is',
    'awesome',
  ],
);

var_dump(
  $tokens
    ->map(
      \ucfirst(...),   // create title case tokens
    )
    ->implode(' '),    // prints "Functional Programming Is Awesome"
);
```

An installation of the bingo-functional library is required to run the code in the example above. Type the following in a console of your choosing to install the library and, with it, the immutable list primitives required for the example.

Installing chemem/bingo-functional via Composer

```
composer require chemem/bingo-functional
```

Persisted in the example are two versions of a special numerically indexed list. The first contains tokens from a phrase and the second title-case versions of the tokens from the first list. This behavior is similar to the preservation of accumulator states in the `Calculator` example, only, instead of numeric values, arrays are preserved.

2.4.2.2 Tries

Tries are generally less popular than immutable lists, but enforce the principle of immutability in more or less the same way. Originally envisioned as an optimal structure for storing strings, the trie (or radix tree) is a persistent tree structure with an empty root node from which child nodes containing lexemes (or characters) sprout. The branching mechanism (or sprouting) inherent in tries is particularly algorithmically effective because it conditions the reuse of nodes and, ultimately, the branches they are a part of. Depending on the word schemes they are created from, nodes in a trie can be reused as parent nodes where there may be lexeme overlaps between words. Tries persist versions of lexemes and particular overlapping sequences across branches for faster traversals. Consider the trie schematic pictured below (Fig. 2.1).

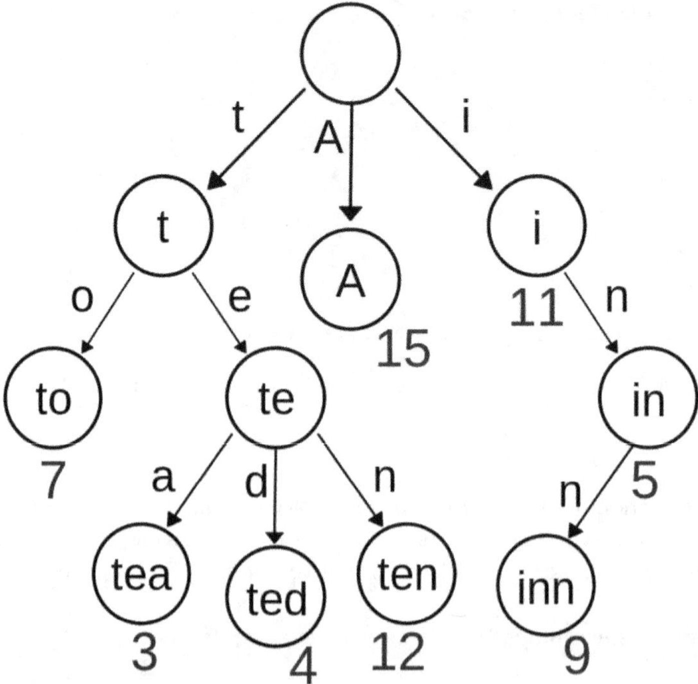

Fig. 2.1 Anatomy of a simple trie

The words stored in the trie pictured above are A, to, tea, ted, ten, i, in, and inn whose corresponding values are 15, 7, 3, 4, 12, 11, 5, and 9, respectively. The cluster of words to, tea, ted, and ten has a common node t; tea, ted, and ten have a common node te; in and inn have a shared lexeme i with in serving as both a stand-alone node and branch predecessor to inn. Traversing the trie to access values assigned to any of the specified keys means navigating branches with reusable nodes in collision-free, alphabetical search operations. Tries are viable alternatives to hashtables, especially in situations where storable keys have similar names. They are used in applications that require elaborate dictionary searches, like phonebooks and spell-checkers.

On the list of PHP's trie implementations are Mark Baker's tries, the `abelzhou/php-trie-tree` and `fran6co/phptrie` packages, and the trie extension. The PECL-installable trie extension, the last option on the shortlist, is particularly interesting as it offers, in addition to regular tries, a more spatially efficient HAT trie, about which more information can be found here. In the example below, a mapping of *Star Wars* characters and their respective affiliations is loaded into a trie, which is then searched for all characters whose names start with the letter L.

Using a trie in PHP

```php
\define('EXIT_FAILURE', 1);

if (!\extension_loaded('php_trie')) {
  echo \sprintf("Please install php_trie to continue\n");
  \exit(EXIT_FAILURE);
}

$trie = HatTrie::fromArray(
  [
    'Leia'         => 'Resistance',
    'Luke'         => 'Jedi',
    'Han Solo'     => 'Resistance',
    'Darth Vader'  => 'Sith',
    'Palpatine'    => 'Sith',
  ],
);

var_dump(
  $trie->prefixSearch('L'),
);
```

Remember to install the extension to perform the featured search via the console directive below.

Installing ext-php_trie via pecl

```
pecl install php_trie
```

2.4.2.3 Temporal Coupling

When implementing persistent structures, it is important to maintain the integrity of their internal states. As established in the previous segment, object modification is only workable when designing for persistence, via method calls that instantiate a reflexive object complete with new property assignments. One of the biggest threats to the integrity of object states, not just in persistent data structures, but also in objects as a whole, is temporal coupling. Objects are considered prone to temporal coupling if their design is such that two or more methods in a chain of method calls are directly bound to each other and, thus, dependent on each other. Temporal coupling creates dependencies that are difficult to separate into distinct chains, as the result of one method call presents a mandatory prerequisite for the successful invocation of its successor. Consider the following rewrite of the recently discussed `Calculator` class.

A version of the Calculator class that is prone to temporal coupling and its side effects

```php
class Calculator
{
  private int $acc;

  public function __construct()
  {
  }

  public function setAcc(int $acc): void
  {
    $this->acc = $acc;
  }

  public function multiply(int $x): void
  {
    $this->acc *= $x;
  }

  public function subtract(int $x): void
  {
    $this->acc -= $x;
  }

  public function value(): int
  {
    return $this->acc;
  }
}

$calc = new Calculator();

$calc->setAcc(0);
$calc->subtract(2);
$calc->multiply(4);

var_dump(
  $calc->value(),
);
```

Every method in the example above, bar the reflective `value` method, functions as a conventional setter. With this version of the `Calculator` class, subtraction and multiplication can only be performed upon the initialization of the accumulator via `setAcc`. Any attempt to perform any of the arithmetic operations defined in the class upon instantiation (via constructor call) produces the following error.

Error message that results from attempting an operation before calling the setAcc method

```
Uncaught Error: Typed property Calculator::$acc must not
be accessed before initialization ...
```

Because an additional call to `setAcc` is required to operationalize the arithmetic operations, the featured version of the `Calculator` class is impure. Every method that is neither the constructor nor the value function updates the internal state of each `Calculator` object spawned from it. As such, creating spin-off chains, and thus new objects, means calling the constructor, `setAcc`, and any series of arithmetic functions—in that order. Objects deemed fit for use in the Functional Programming paradigm do not require long additional initialization chains upon instantiation and can easily be spun off into distinct chains.

> Read-Only Classes

Introduced in PHP 8.2, read-only classes make it easy to implement persistent data structures in the language, for they are designed to enforce immutability. Placing values in a read-only class is only doable on instantiation by default. As such, method chain calls in read-only objects cannot be temporally coupled. All that is required to create a read-only class is the keyword, which, when prepended to a class definition, effectively designates it as such.

Template for creating persistent objects from readonly classes in PHP 8.2+

```
readonly class Calculator
{
  /* pure class implementation */
}

$result = (new Calculator())
  ->subtract(2)
  ->multiply(4)
  ->value();

echo $result;
```

While it is not impossible to create pure objects from regular classes, as in previous segments, read-only classes best enforce the rules of object purity and can be seen as a means of testing whether those rules hold. Moving forward, all persistent class artifacts, that is, classes from which persistent objects can be created, will demonstrably be coded as read-only.

This second chapter is effectively complete. It is highly likely that its exploration of the concepts of pure functions, referential transparency, and immutability has enhanced the appeal of the Functional Programming paradigm. The focus of the next chapter, composition, builds on the concepts described in this one and introduces reusable patterns that can be readily inserted into everyday code.

Chapter 3
Composition

3.1 The Basics

Composition can be intuitively considered a form of function husbandry wherein function calls are organized into a linear sequence such that each call counts as a transformative step in an elaborate algorithm. The composition in computer programming is very similar to that in Mathematics. In a situation where two unary functions are presented—one $f(x)$ that increments the number passed to it by one and another $g(x)$ that computes the square of its sole argument—a composition $g \circ f$ such that the numerical input of $f(x)$ is incremented and then subsequently squared can be created where necessary: where the *afore*established order is required. This can be represented notationally as follows.

$$f(x) = x + 1 \tag{3.1}$$

$$g(x) = x^2 \tag{3.2}$$

$$g \circ f = (x + 1)^2 \tag{3.3}$$

The composition above, but really composition as a whole, is congruous with the Lambda Calculus, as the β-conversion allows for it. The featured version of $g \circ f$ is encodable in the Lambda Calculus as

$$f = \lambda x[x + 1] \tag{3.4}$$

$$g = \lambda x[x^2] \tag{3.5}$$

$$g \circ f = \lambda g.\lambda f.\lambda x[g(fx)] \, or \, \lambda g f x[g(fx)] \tag{3.6}$$

© The Author(s), under exclusive license to APress Media, LLC,
part of Springer Nature 2026
M. B. Lochemem, *Functional Programming in PHP*,
https://doi.org/10.1007/979-8-8688-2468-5_3

In substituting the variables g and f with the parameterized expressions they are assigned, per the conventions of the β-conversion, it is possible to arrive at the final applicatory form of $g \circ f$ from earlier.

$$g \circ f = \lambda g f x[g(fx)] \tag{3.7}$$

$$= \lambda g x[g(x+1)] \tag{3.8}$$

$$= \lambda x[(x+1)^2] \tag{3.9}$$

The derived compact representation of the identity $g \circ f$ can be, in a subsequent β-conversion, applied to a numeric value such as 2, for instance, as in the example below.

$$g \circ f = (\lambda x[(x+1)^2])2 \triangleright (2+1)^2 \tag{3.10}$$

$$= 9 \tag{3.11}$$

Algorithmically, composition creates meta-functions from functions organized in a linear sequence. A fitting mechanical allegory for composition is the action of using a chain hoist to lift a heavy weight. In the allegory, the weight lifting is the algorithm for which the chain is the means through which to apply a force to lift the weight—the meta-function. The links in the chain are the function constituents of the algorithm and thence the sequenced cogs through which a transmittable hoisting force is applied. In computer programming, composing functions can be done in either a traditional, commonplace way or in a nuanced, point-free style that is similar to the mathematical approach described thus far.

3.2 Traditional Composition

If a PHP program contains functions, there is a high chance that at least some of them are contextually chainable. If the formable chains can be written so as to look like nested function calls, with the bottommost (or rightmost) being the first in the sequence and the topmost (or leftmost) being the last in the same sequence, then they can be considered traditional. This approach to composing functions is almost second nature for the average PHP programmer, regardless of whether they are versed in the principles of Functional Programming or not. Imagine a program that converts a title interspersed in some markup to a slug appendable to the path of a URL. A traditional composition like the one featured in the example below is workable in such a program to the extent of capturing the entire conversion mechanism.

Traditional composition in PHP

```
\define(
  'TITLE',
  <<<'HTML'
  <h2>
    Chaining is Composing
  </h2>
  HTML,
);

// convert spaces to hyphens
$slug = \preg_replace(
  '/(\s){1,}/',
  '-',
  // trim whitespace
  \trim(
    // remove markup tags
    \strip_tags(TITLE),
  ),
);

echo $slug . PHP_EOL;
```

The PHP interpreter **eagerly** evaluates the expression assigned to $slug—from bottom to top. It first removes all markup tags and trims the whitespace in the resultant string before ultimately replacing all spaces in the penultimate string output with hyphens. For the traditional composition shown above to work, all relevant arguments must be passed to each function discriminately. While such an approach works almost every time the said arguments are at the ready, it makes for some awfully long, hard-to-read chains in situations where multiple function calls are linearly sequenced. A style better suited to lazily controlling program flow and, with it, the sequence of successive function applications might prove useful in such cases.

3.3 Point-Free Composition

An alternative to traditional composition, the point-free style is an approach to composing functions that is less frequently discussed in PHP. When using the point-free style, it is imperative to think explicitly of the combinable rules in a chain, and thus the functions that represent them, and implicitly about their arguments. While function parameters are ultimately important, the point-free approach stresses that they need not be ignored, but rather, thought of as data that constitute the chain in which they reside. As such, the point-free style manifests as a pseudo-list of functions (often function names) whose execution order is (normatively) that of the contiguous entries in the list. It is prone to producing computational equivalents of the mathematical compositions from a previous segment and works best when all the functions in a chain are unary. A stylistically appropriate rewrite of the previous markup-to-slug converter would look like the following.

Point-free composition in PHP

```
use function Chemem\Bingo\Functional\compose;

$slug = compose(
  \strip_tags(...),
  \trim(...),
  fn (string $input): string =>
    \preg_replace(
      '/(\s){1,}/',
      '_',
      $input,
    ),
);

echo $slug(TITLE);
```

The chain from before, in the snippet above, is a more compact pseudo-list of functions assigned to the variable `$slug`. The said list is a more legible ordering of the functions from the previous example that are combined into a single callable unit via the function `compose`. `compose` behaves in the same way as the pipe operator, a feature slated to debut in PHP in version 8.5 and a mainstay in languages like Haskell, OCaml, and F#. It is a meta-utility in PHP that performs a series of β-conversions on functions in a chain, for it propagates the output of one function to the next. Point-free composition creates a single meta-function that can be abstracted over a single argument—the markup containing the title, in this case. It is a means of elegantly defining unary meta-rules: higher-order abstractions of linearly sequenced functions.

Furthermore, point-free compositions are associative. Associativity is a fundamental principle underlying binary operations such as chain addition and chain multiplication. It renders the results of such operations immune to changes from logical groupings, notationally represented as parenthetical separation of adjacent suboperations. The expression $(2+2)+2$, for instance, always evaluates to 6 as the grouping $(2 + 2)$ yields no tangible expression-breaking result and is interpretable as $2 + 2 + 2$. Like the chains in persistent objects, those written in a point-free style can be spun off into smaller chains similar to the aforediscussed logical groupings, if their overall orderings of rules (functions) do not change. If there were ever to arise a need to combine steps 1 and 2 from the conversion algorithm shown earlier, the resultant hypothetical composition would not break the converter.

Demonstration of the associativity of point-free composition

```
$slug = compose(
  // sub-chain with steps 1 and 2 from before
  fn (string $markup): string =>
    compose(
      \strip_tags(...),
      \trim(...),
    )($markup),
  fn (string $input): string =>
    \preg_replace(
      '/(\s){1,}/',
      '_',
      $input,
    ),
);

echo $slug(TITLE); // same result as before
```

Spin-off chains in more elaborate sequences can create more readable compositions, especially if sequestered in functions placed in separate files. Debugging faults in such chains reduces the possibility of errors such as the propagation of invalid data between function applications (or β-conversions) or runtime-halting exceptions occurring in the larger chains they are a part of. For all the perks of point-free composition, there is one glaring downside that stems from the technique's incompatibility with functions that are not unary. Such a flaw would otherwise be damning for the point-free style if lazy control flow via higher-order functions were not achievable within PHP.

3.4 Higher-Order Functions

Functions are first-class citizens in PHP. They can be plugged into many contexts in much the same way as more commonplace primitive data structures—integers, strings, and the like. Functions can be treated as arguments by other functions, returned at the end of a function signature as an atomic value, or both. The callable units that utilize any of these strategies are referred to as higher-order functions and can effect a lazy flow control via function application. Such functions make it possible to sequence successive evaluations and confer the ability to access them in an ad hoc way because the expressions that reside in the signatures of functions are only evaluated by the interpreter when all of their relevant parameters are provided. To demonstrate this laziness, a reimagined version of the converter should suffice.

The markup-to-title converter reimagined as a higher-order function

```php
function markup2title(string $title): callable
{
  // strip tags from the original input
  $stripped = \strip_tags($title);

  // optionally remove whitespace at the beginning and end of
  the string  return function (bool $trim) use ($stripped):
  callable {    $trimmed = $trim ? \trim($stripped) :
  $stripped;

    // optionally create title-case version
    return fn (bool $titlecase): string =>
      \preg_replace(
        '/(\s){1,}/',
        '_',
        $titlecase ?
          \implode(
            ' ',
            \array_map(
              \ucfirst(...),
              \preg_split('/(\s)/', $trimmed),
            ),
          ) :
          $trimmed,
      );
  };
}
```

In the reimagined version, the conversion process consists of three steps. The first is the stripping of tags from the input string, the second is the optional trimming of whitespace at the beginning and end of the stripped output, and the third and final step features the conversion of spaces to hyphens, with an optional conversion of each word to its title-case equivalent—a string with the first letter capitalized. Each of the aforelisted steps constitutes a phase in a linear, three-step execution plan that, from a control flow perspective, **does not** need to follow the one that precedes it in immediate succession. If, between two successive calls, some data relevant to the next call were to be introduced, it would be, per the intent of lazy evaluation, passed to the next function in the call sequence. Consider the following lazy conversion.

Lazy conversion with the reimagined markup-to-tile converter

```php
\define(
  'TITLE',
  '<h2>Higher-order functions confer lazy flow control</h2>',
);
```

```
// strip tags from title
$strip   = markup2title(TITLE);

// trim only if the string length is greater than 10
$trim    = $strip(
  \mb_strlen(TITLE) > 10,
);

// assign base URL
$baseurl = 'https://awesomeblog.net';
// compute title case format of slug only in the event that
the host is a .com domain
$slug    = $trim(
  \preg_match(
    '/^(.*)(\.){1}(.com){1}$/',
    \parse_url($baseurl)['host'],
  ),
);

// append slug to base URL
echo \sprintf(
  "%s/%s\n",
  $baseurl,
  $slug,
);
```

Between steps 1 and 2 shown above, the interpreter eagerly checks if the title length is greater than 10 before passing the output of the logical operation to the second function in the sequence. Then, between steps 2 and 3, it performs a base URL assignment before computing a slug, the words in which are converted to their title-case equivalents only on condition that the URL to which it is ultimately appended contains a .com domain. The aforedescribed operations are stand-ins for real-world computations that could potentially occur between successive applications in a higher-order function setup. Higher-order functions effect a deferrable composition because all calls in the sequences described in their signatures can be instated as needed. Further still, breaking down the converter into function applications that each complete a necessary step in the conversion process and are usable in an ad hoc fashion effectively hints at the ability to decompose functions and, thus, a means to achieve a point-free composition via lazy flow control.

3.5 Currying

Lazy evaluation via higher-order functions, for all its perks, is unworkable in programs where the only option for function decomposition is manual. Changing the complexion of functions to produce multi-step function applications, as in the reimagined converter, can become a strenuous activity, since most functions that take more than a single argument are just fine in their respective constitutions. Such functions can, however, be molded into lazily evaluable higher-order functions, much in the same way as unary functions can be sequenced in a chain, in relevant order of application—via a meta-technique and, thus, a meta-utility. The technique through which to convert n-ary functions to unary ones is called currying. Currying is a means of decomposing functions that take multiple arguments into smaller subfunctions that each take a single argument. Yet another rewrite of the markup-to-slug converter, this time a function that takes three arguments and encodes the same ideas as the higher-order version in the previous segment, is a great fit for demonstrating the effectiveness of currying.

The markup-to-title converter rewritten as a ternary function

```php
use function Chemem\Bingo\Functional\compose;

function markup2title(
  string $title,
  bool $trim,
  bool $titlecase,
): string {
  return compose(
    \strip_tags(...),
    fn (string $stripped): string =>
      $trim ?
        \trim($stripped) :
        $stripped,
    fn (string $trimmed): string =>
      \preg_replace(
        '/(\s){1,}/',
        '_',
        $titlecase ?
          \implode(
            ' ',
            \array_map(
              \ucfirst(...),
              \preg_split('/(\s)/', $trimmed),
            ),
          ) :
          $trimmed,
      ),
  )($title);
}
```

Passing the function above as the sole argument to the function curry, a utility that, like compose, effects a meta-functionality like the technique it is named after, decomposes the converter and thence creates the higher-order function from before.

Decomposing the ternary converter with the curry function

```
use function Chemem\Bingo\Functional\curry;

$convert = curry(markup2title(...));
```

The same laziness demonstrated in the previous segment applies to the new curried converter. The curry utility ensures that the string result in the rewritten converter, ordinarily attainable in a single call, can only be achieved after three ordered, ad hoc function applications, each an abstraction over a single value. As far as point-free composition goes, a post-conversion step, appending a generated slug to a URL, also showcased earlier, can be added to a chain that starts with the final call to a decomposed converter. Take a look at the snippet below.

Recreating lazy evaluation with a curried converter

```
use function Chemem\Bingo\Functional\{
  compose,
  curry,
};

$convert = curry(markup2title(...));
$strip   = $convert(TITLE);

$trim    = $strip(
  \mb_strlen(TITLE) > 10,
);

$baseurl = 'https://awesomeblog.net';
$tourl   = compose(
  $trim,
  fn (string $input): string =>
    \sprintf(
      '%s/%s',
      $baseurl,
      $input,
    ),
);

echo $tourl(
  \preg_match(
    '/^(.*)(\.){1}(.com){1}$/',
    \parse_url($baseurl)['host'],
  ),
) . PHP_EOL;
```

Circumvented in the example is the glaring limitation of the point-free style. In decomposing the converter, a usable unary function is lazily created before it is plugged into a linear sequence. Currying simultaneously creates more composable functions and offers a means of applying abstractions over arguments as needed. In functional languages like Haskell, for instance, the technique is a focal point of the compiler such that all functions in the language's userspace are curried by default. In PHP, where the necessary compiler optimizations that enable default currying behavior are mostly absent and internal plumbing is required to produce function decomposition, the laziness inherent to currying is mostly optional, as is that tied to another concept that produces subfunctions of slightly bigger arities— partial application.

3.6 Partial Application

Often, the most prudent decomposition strategy in a multi-step, lazy algorithm is one that accounts for the presence of some, but not all, arguments of an n-ary function at different points in a program's flow. This contrasts with the conditions ideal for currying that strictly require successive abstractions over a single value and therefore induce a strict unary form. Partial application is a versatile approach to decomposition wherein subfunctions that take one or more arguments can be spawned from a single function with an accommodatingly large arity. Passing the same converter used in the previous segment to the utility `partial`, as in the example to follow, unlocks permutations of lazily evaluable sequenced function applications.

Decomposing the ternary converter with the partial function

```
use function Chemem\Bingo\Functional\partial;

$convert = partial(
  markup2title(...),
  TITLE,
  \mb_strlen(TITLE) > 10,
);
```

If there is a need to continue with the same currying pattern from before, partial application will enable it. If more than one viable argument materializes between successive applications, however, a decomposition that allows for abstraction over more than one argument is also workable.

Creating a terser lazy evaluation with a partially-applied converter

```php
use function Chemem\Bingo\Functional\{
  compose,
  partial,
};

$convert = partial(
  markup2title(...),
  TITLE,
  \mb_strlen(TITLE) > 10,
);

$baseurl = 'https://awesomeblog.com';
$tourl   = compose(
  $trim,
  fn (string $input): string =>
    \sprintf(
      '%s/%s',
      $baseurl,
      $input,
    ),
);

echo $tourl(
  \preg_match(
    '/^(.*)(\.){1}(.com){1}$/',
    \parse_url($baseurl)['host'],
  ),
) . PHP_EOL;
```

The example above demonstrates a scenario in which the title and the computation of its length can be presented in one step before the slug is ultimately computed in the last function application, which is deferrable to the point after a URL is defined and a decision is made based on its domain. The resultant unary function from the application of two arguments in one go is just as usable in a point-free chain designed to append a slug to a URL as that from the previous example, which was arrived at after two deferred applications of unary functions. Partial application is a wonderful feature that can help create situationally suitable, creative flow control options.

3.7 Map, Filter, and Fold

Higher-order functions increase the potential for function application and, therefore, make programs more amenable to function composition. The aforediscussed decomposition renders functions composable in discretionary ways that circumvent the eagerness of the PHP interpreter, but is not the only enhancement associated with such artifacts. In map, filter, and fold are higher-order functions that extend the applicability of functions, but more specifically the expressions that encode the rules they implement, to various data encapsulated in composite structures. `map`, `filter`, and `fold` are generally thought of as conducive to processing data in lists—arrays, hashtables, vectors, and the like—but they also apply to more nuanced structures too, as you, the reader, will find out in future chapters. In this segment, the respective discussions on each of the aforelisted patterns center around each pattern's applicability to processing list data.

3.7.1 Map

Fundamentally, the map operation enables the application of a single function to all data within a modifiable structure. As far as lists are concerned, this application is performed on all their constituent elements in a single iteration and produces new lists, the contents of which are the results of each modificative application. PHP's `array_map` function is a go-to for most mapping operations that involve hashtables. To follow is a demonstration of the pattern's usage on a list of integers.

Performing a map operation with array_map

```
\var_dump(
  \array_map(
    $fib = fn (int $val) use (&$fib): int {
      return $val < 2 ?
        $val :
        $fib($val - 2) + $fib($val - 1);
    },
    \range(4, 8),
  ),
);
```

The map operation shown produces a list that resembles a Fibonacci sequence for integers in the range 6–10. In one pass through the hashtable, the `array_map` function computes the Fibonacci number for each entry and places it in a new hashtable. `array_map` also offers the ability to apply the expressions defined in a single function to multiple arrays. This optional feature can be utilized to create a hashtable that is a mapping of an arbitrary set of keys to a list of numbers within the specified range—effectively, a mimicry of the binary `array_combine` function.

Mimicking the behavior of array_combine with array_map

```php
$fib = function (int $val) use (&$fib): int {
  return $val < 2 ?
    $val :
    $fib($val - 2) + $fib($val - 1);
};

$seq = \array_merge(
  ...[
    ...\array_map(
      fn (int $value, string $key): array =>
      [$key => $fib($value)],
      \range(4, 8),
      [
        'foo',
        'bar',
        'baz',
        'qux',
        'quux',
      ],
    ),
  ],
);

\var_dump($seq);
```

Unfortunately, the use of `array_map` is limited to arrays only. While this might not be a problem in situations in which hashtables are a focal point, it most certainly is otherwise, especially when some kind of traversable object is used in lieu of a hashtable. To mitigate the aforestated problem is the utility `map`, also included in the bingo-functional library, that works on both objects and hashtables. If the same array of numbers were sequenced in a traversable instance of the `stdClass`, for example, computing a derivative list of Fibonacci numbers would be done with `map`, like so.

Transforming an object with a more versatile map function

```php
use function Chemem\Bingo\Functional\map;

$modified = map($fib, (object) \range(4, 8));

var_dump($modified);
```

`map` can generally be considered an "apply-to-all" operation that characteristically returns the same contextual type, in this case, a hashtable or traversable object, as that provided to it as an argument.

3.7.2 *Filter*

The filter operation allows for the exclusion of data from a composite structure that do not satisfy a condition that would qualify their inclusion in a forward-propagated version of that structure. Filtering out is essentially removing items in a list—or a similar structure—that fail some arbitrary logical test, items that, when substituted for in an expression that should evaluate to true, evaluate to false. Much like the apply-to-all mapping operation discussed in the previous segment, filtering occurs in a single iteration—in a single pass through a composite structure—and thence returns a new list containing items that satisfy a logical condition. The `array_filter` operation is a commonplace userland solution for all filtering that involves hashtables. Consider the filter to follow.

Performing a filter operation with array_filter

```
$characters = [
  'Spiderman' => 'Avenger',
  'Ironman' => 'Avenger',
  'Black Widow' => 'Avenger',
  'Baron Zemo' => 'Sokovian',
  'Red Skull' => 'Hydra',
];

$avengers = \array_filter(
  $characters,
  fn (string $affiliation): bool =>
    (bool) \preg_match('/^(avenger)$/i', $affiliation),
);

var_dump($avengers);
```

The featured filter removes, from a hashtable containing names and affiliations of Marvel characters, all entries, and thus names of characters, not designated as Avengers. It creates a new, smaller list from an iterative evaluation of a boolean predicate—the regular expression that serves as an encoding of the aforestated affiliation test. Because `array_filter` also supports filtering exclusively by key, or both key and value, the examples below, each relevant to the same character list but representative of a different filter criterion, are valid.

Creating filters with specialized array_filter options

```
$men = \array_filter(
  $characters,
  fn (string $key): bool => (bool) \preg_match('/(men)$/',
  $key),
  ARRAY_FILTER_USE_KEY,
);

$sokovian = \array_filter(
  $characters,
  fn (string $value, string $key): bool =>
    (bool) \preg_match('/(Zemo)/', $key) &&
    (bool) \preg_match('/(Sokovia)/', $value),
  ARRAY_FILTER_USE_BOTH,
);

var_dump(
  $men,
  $sokovian,
);
```

The first filter operation in the example above creates a new list of characters whose names have a "man" in them, and the second filters out all characters that neither are Sokovian nor have the name "Baron Zemo." Although the filters above are rather elaborate, they only apply to hashtables, much like `array_map` from the preceding segment. filter, yet another utility in the bingo-functional library, extends each of the aforedescribed features to traversable objects that could just as well contain the same base character data. Take the following recreation of a recently showcased filter operation.

Filtering out elements of an object with a versatile filter function

```
use function Chemem\Bingo\Functional\filter;

$characters                = new stdClass();
$characters->{'Spiderman'}  = 'Avenger';
$characters->{'Ironman'}    = 'Avenger';
$characters->{'Black Widow'} = 'Avenger';
$characters->{'Baron Zemo'}  = 'Sokovian';
$characters->{'Red Skull'}   = 'Hydra';

var_dump(
  filter(
    fn (string $value, string $key): bool =>
      (bool) \preg_match('/(Zemo)/', $key) &&
      (bool) \preg_match('/(Sokovia)/', $value),
```

```
      $characters,
      ARRAY_FILTER_USE_BOTH,
    ),
  );
```

Selecting the character "Baron Zemo" from a list fashioned as an object with dynamic keys follows largely the same conventions used in the filter it mimics. Generally, the filter pattern allows for the creation of expressions that implement its "remove-if" rule and should be considered whenever a situation calls for the truncation of a data structure compatible with it.

3.7.3   Fold

Perhaps the most versatile of the trio of higher-order functions discussed in this section of the chapter, fold is a pattern that allows for the transformation of a composite structure into a single value. Otherwise referred to as reduce, fold is a higher-order function that, in a single iteration through a list, combines each result of each successive function application on each list entry into an accumulator. The fold operation updates the said accumulator to which a value is assigned at the start of the iteration it performs, through its every step. The final accumulator value the pattern produces is the result of several successive updates, the type of which is typically that of the initial value passed to it as an argument. Depending on the demands of the situation for which fold is deemed sufficient, the accumulator could be of any type, provided the modifications made to it through the steps of the pattern's intrinsic iteration are compatible with that type. Most userspace types are manipulable with fold for this reason, and the pattern is, therefore, a wellspring of sub-patterns and iterative designs catered to highly specialized use cases. One such use case is the min operation shown below.

Mimicking the behavior of the min function with array_reduce

```
$min = \array_reduce(
  [12, 22, -1, -33, 447],
  function (int $acc, int $next): int {
    $acc = $next < $acc ? $next : $acc;

    return $acc;
  },
  0,
);

var_dump($min);
```

The featured application of `array_reduce`, the native PHP function with which to apply fold operations to hashtables, is such that in each step of the ensuing iteration, the list item subject to function application, an integer in the specified list of integers, has its magnitude compared with that of the value assigned to the accumulator at a corresponding phase of the iteration. This comparison is performed via the phased application of a special callback called a reducer, wherein all the necessary modificative expressions reside.

In the version of `min` implemented above, the accumulator is iteratively, situationally assigned the value adjudged to have the lowest magnitude of the two operands in the logical comparison defined in the reducer. With each step, the accumulator either retains the value from that which precedes it or takes on the result of a different comparison. Because the accumulator is a stateful element modified through successive operational updates, it is possible to track its forms through the steps that update it, in some secondary list. Such tracking can be implemented like so.

Tracking accumulator modifications in a custom version of the min function

```php
[
  'history' => $history,
  'min'     => $min,
] = \array_reduce(
  [12, 22, -1, -33, 447],
  function (array $acc, int $next): array {
    $acc['history'] = $acc['min'];
    $acc['min']     = $next < $acc['min'] ? $next : $acc['min'];

    return $acc;
  },
  [
    'history' => [],
    'min'     => 0,
  ],
);

var_dump($history, $min);
```

The list that contains all update history, appropriately named `$history`, is effectively a log of all accumulator values through each step of the iteration in the min operation, recorded before each comparison and subsequent update. If such behavior looks familiar, it is likely because state tracking is a fixture in state management toolkits like Redux and flow control patterns inherent to syntaxes like Elm. Such tools impose on those who use them a means of managing state in composite list structures via fold-powered state machines and, consequently, elaborate reducers.

Because the applicative potential of fold is not constrained to basic primitives, the pattern's reach can be expanded to create more avenues for function application—patterns that are themselves higher-order functions. For such patterns to materialize, the iteration inherent in the fold operation must be configured so as to produce functions. map, filter, and the point-free compose function, all patterns that have been covered thus far, can each be derived from a single fold function call. In fact, they are all often written as derivatives of the fold pattern in userspace libraries such as bingo-functional.

When deriving the map operation from a single fold call, the primary concern is ensuring that the accumulator, instantiated as a list whose type matches that of the artifact passed to the function as an argument, is modified iteratively such that each new entry is a version of the item in the list subject to traversal modified by a discretionarily chosen unary function, also passed to the map function as an argument. A userspace map function can be fashioned from a fold operation like this.

Deriving a map function from an invocation of fold

```
use function Chemem\Bingo\Functional\fold;

function map(callable $function, array $list): array
{
  return fold(
    function (
      array $acc,
      mixed $next,
      string $key,
    ) use ($function): array {
      $acc[$key] = $function($next);

      return $acc;
    },
    $list,
    [],
  );
}
```

A derivative filter function is a little different. Instead of being written to add function-modified versions of target list entries to the accumulator on each iteration, the callback passed to fold is written so as to only add to the accumulator entries that produce truthy values once abstracted over by a unary function. Something like the following suffices to this end.

Deriving a filter function from an invocation of fold

```php
use function Chemem\Bingo\Functional\fold;

function filter(callable $function, array $list): array
{
  return fold(
    function (
      array $acc,
      mixed $next,
      string $key,
    ) use ($function): array {
      if ($function($next)) {
        $acc[$key] = $next;
      }

      return $acc;
    },
    $list,
    [],
  );
}
```

To derive a compose function, a higher-order callback is required. Achieving the kind of forward chaining described earlier in this chapter is possible if, first, the list through which to iterate contains only unary functions; if, second, the accumulator is initially assigned an identity function to set off a chain of successive function applications; and if, third and finally, the callback is itself a higher-order function such that the argument eventually passed to the meta one is, when provided, first applied to the most recent accumulator function and then to the next in the list of functions. In this way, compose is lazily evaluated, that is, at the juncture where the sole argument to transform through a series of applications is passed to it. The function below implements a point-free composition that is usable in the manner advertised earlier in the chapter.

Deriving a function composition (compose) utility from an invocation of fold

```php
use function Chemem\Bingo\Functional\fold;

function compose(callable ...$functions): callable
{
  return fold(
    $functions,
    fn (callable $acc, callable $next): callable =>
      fn (mixed $val): mixed =>
        $next(
          $acc($val),
```

```
        ),
    fn (mixed $x): mixed => $x,
  );
}
```

With all fold operations, the throughline is a phased accumulator modification with a reducer. While in most practical use cases, such as those demonstrated thus far, only a single reducer is required, there exists a possibility of chaining reducers with fold. This technique, achievable with some extra plumbing, renders patterns like the aforedescribed map and filter, as well as those similar to them, chainable in a single iteration.

3.7.3.1   Transducers

A transducer is a list data processing pipeline. Transducers are extensions of the fold pattern. They allow those who use them to create composable reducers that combine one or more list-modifying functions, such as the aforediscussed map and filter, in a single iteration, without producing any intermediate lists. When presented with a list of integers and two successive operations on the said list—one a map that squares each number in it and the next a filter that extracts all the multiples of three from the list of squares, for instance—the most instinctive way to express the aforedescribed transformations is to write them like so.

Sequencing map and filter operations

```
use function Chemem\Bingo\Functional\{
  filter,
  map,
};

$list = \range(1, 20);

// generates list containing squares of numbers in list
$square = map(
  fn (int $x): int => \pow($x, 2),
  $list,
);

// generates list containing multiples of 3
$multiples = filter(
  fn (int $x): bool => equals($x % 3, 0),
  $square,
);

var_dump(
  $square,
```

```
  $multiples,
);
```

While the expressions above are perfectly valid, they each create a separate list
from a distinct iteration. The temporal costs of two separate iterations through two
small lists like the ones featured in the example might be considered tolerable,
but could pose a challenge when larger lists containing, say, multiple thousands
of entries are to be funneled into the same map-then-filter series of higher-order
function applications. With a transducer, it is possible not only to mitigate the
potential temporal inefficiencies from separate phased modifications of large lists
but also to create elaborate reducers that feature succinct expressions of modificative
operations in a point-free style. Consider the following rewrite.

Chaining map and filter operations with a transducer

```
use function Chemem\Bingo\Functional\{
  Transducer\filter,
  Transducer\map,
  compose,
  equals,
  fold,
  transduce,
};

$reducer = compose(
  map(
    fn (int $x): int => \pow($x, 2),
  ),
  filter(
    fn (int $x): bool => equals($x % 3, 0),
  ),
);

var_dump(
  transduce(
    $reducer,
    fn (
      array $acc,
      int $val,
      string|int $key,
    ): array => [...$acc, $key => $val],
    $list,
    [],
  ),
);
```

The map and filter operations from earlier are, in the rewrite above, represented as compact higher-order forms. Each of these forms is unary and takes a single relevant modificative callback. Chaining the said forms into a meta-function via `compose` effects a transducer function, the quintessential pipeline function with which to shape the order of transformation. The transducer is only one part of the meta-reducer implemented by the `transduce` utility, the chainable part. It lacks the syntactic vigor with which to update the accumulator in each step of the ensuing iteration and is therefore complemented by the step function, the callback that follows it, whose purpose is to guarantee the propagation of all valid accumulator states at each step. As far as the above rewrite is concerned, a concatenation of a previous list with the entries that would ultimately constitute the next one ultimately proves sufficient. Applying the transducer to the step function, or intuitively chaining the latter and the former, produces the meta-reducer ultimately passed to the fold function in the signature of `transduce`.

Intuitively, the transduce operation depicted above can be described as the phased application of relevant map and filter operations, in succession, to each item in a 20-item-long list of integers. With transducers, and in particular the higher-order functions used in conjunction with them, the lists that would otherwise be generated in distinct steps are a non-factor. Such is the effectiveness of the pattern.

This marks the conclusion of the third chapter of this book and, thus, the primer on composing functions in PHP. The next chapter is structured in such a way as to provide insights into handling errors, inevitabilities that negatively impact the efficacy of computer programs, with techniques congruent with composition.

Chapter 4
Error Handling

4.1 Exceptions

Exceptions are artifacts that are designed to represent abnormal occurrences in computer programs. Their significance is in capturing all data relevant to a failure, typically of the critical kind, and relaying it when a failure precondition is met. In PHP, exceptions are artifacts that behave differently under different conditions: as objects in transit and at rest and as runtime halters when explicitly thrown. An exception object, like that shown in the snippet to follow, subsumes error-related properties and read-only methods.

A simple Exception object

```php
$exception = new Exception('An error occurred!');

echo $exception->getMessage() . PHP_EOL;
```

Such objects, like those discussed in Chapter 2, are assignable and can be shuttled around in much the same way as functions or variables. When used in a throw expression, they force the termination of a program and condition the display of all (mostly read-only) error information contained within them. The following example demonstrates this behavior.

© The Author(s), under exclusive license to APress Media, LLC, part of Springer Nature 2026
M. B. Lochemem, *Functional Programming in PHP*,
https://doi.org/10.1007/979-8-8688-2468-5_4

A function designed to conditionally throw an Exception on invocation

```
function add(int $x, int $y): int
{
  if (!($x > 10 || $y > 10)) {
    throw new Exception(
      \sprintf('One of the arguments has a magnitude lower
      than 10'),
    );
  }

  return $x + $y;
}

echo add(2, 15);
```

In the signature of yet another variation of the add function from Chapter 1, the sum of two integers is only computed if both function arguments evaluated inside of it have a magnitude greater than 10. The failure, effectively triggered when the function is invoked with the arguments 2 and 15, stops the runtime, preempting further execution: the interpreter terminates the program and displays a rich text containing a message summary, file and line numbers instructive in so far as pinpointing the origin of the causal throw expression, and a stack trace with which to track the causal error sequence every entry in which shows all afflicted files. The following message is the output of the errant call.

Message written to an output device when exception is thrown

```
PHP Fatal error:  Uncaught Exception: One of the arguments has
a magnitude lower than 10 in file.php:6
Stack trace:
#0 file.php(14): add()
#1 {main}
  thrown in file.php on line 6
```

Because no value is returned when the runtime is halted, and the rule that mandates an integer be returned from an operation on two integer arguments is broken, the thrown exception breaks referential transparency. Seeing as exceptions generally behave in the manner depicted, when thrown, it is valid to conclude that they violate the Dao of Functional Programming: they are irreconcilable with type signatures and, thus, the rules that define the functions in which they are thrown. The inevitability of errors and the tendency to throw exceptions in PHP to account for them necessitate the use of strategies that simultaneously minimize halting behavior and retain all relevant error information. The rest of the chapter details such strategies that can either be combined or used separately.

4.2 Callbacks

Callbacks are functions that can be passed as arguments to other functions. They effect higher-order function patterns similar to those discussed in the previous chapter and can replace exceptions when explicitly tailored to handle error conditions that would otherwise be represented in throw expressions. When invoked in a manner that remedies an error condition with the correct error state, a callback can be especially useful in preventing the runtime from coming to a standstill due to a thrown exception. A version of the head function from earlier that only extracts the first value from a hashtable containing numeric keys, that is, the value accessible via the index 0, can be written, as in the snippet to follow, in such a way as to accept a callback whose purpose is handling the error that could result from the absence of a value whose slot index is the same as the aforespecified.

A binary head function that takes a callback function as an argument

```
function head(array $list, callable $callback): mixed
{
  return $list[0] ?? $callback($list);
}
```

In the function shown above, a callback is invoked with the hashtable passed to it as a sole parameter, in the event that the index 0 does not exist in the said list. Herein lies an opportunity to remedy potential failure via function application. One way to fashion a callback fit for purpose is to parameterize an appropriate sequence of expressions better suited to extracting the first element in both an object and a hashtable, with the aim of retrieving a more accurate result. The following can prove sufficient in this regard.

A callback that can be passed to the reimagined head function

```
$callback = function (array $list): mixed {
  \reset($list);

  $result = \current($list);

  return !$result ? null : $result;
};
```

The callback shown above avoids a dreaded throw expression by enhancing the retrieval capabilities of the function in which it is ultimately called on detection of an error. If passed to the head function with a list that does not contain the required index, as in the first of two examples to follow, the first value of the list, the string value "foo," is retrieved. In a situation in which there are no values in a hashtable, as in the second example in the snippet below, the fully applied head expression evaluates to the primitive null, indicating the absence of an appropriate value.

Handling errors with a callback

```
var_dump(
  // example 1
  head(
    [
      'foo' => 'foo',
      'bar' => 12,
      'baz' => 3.3312,
    ],
    $callback,
  ),
  // example 2
  head([], $callback),
);
```

In neither of the cases depicted above is the runtime halted. The callback used in each case above propagates a value compatible with the signature of the function of which it is a parameter whenever a failure occurs. Because it is possible to forgo the computational rigor in the callback featured thus far and tighten restrictions on the head function in such a way as to return a singular value, null, once failure is encountered, a callback variant like the one below can also suffice.

Callback that returns null

```
$callback = fn (mixed $_): mixed => null;
```

The succinct version shown above only serves to highlight the tunability of callbacks, as it too does not break referential transparency but rather enforces a strictness that effects a binary logic, effectively ensuring that all expressions that feature lists lacking the index 0 evaluate to null. Because of this tunability, callbacks can be used to create error resolution patterns within functions that allow for the use of enhancive hyperintensional forms where they can be applied, complementary expressions compatible with overall function signatures whenever warranted, but also appropriate (often scalar) values where necessary.

Although callbacks can be versatile, they are at times difficult to weave into functions that can be written to accommodate them, as picking the right parameters to forward to them can be a challenge at times. While the first callback showcased in this segment offered error handling in the form of an enhancement of the core expression in the function in which it was invoked, the second needed no such consideration, as no argument was required. Though trivial and often circumvented by PHP's weak typing system that ignores arguments in callbacks, the said problem might present readability and enhancement problems where a standardized callback pattern does not exist.

Further still, because callbacks are best expressed in succinct forms, they can, when written so as to include other more elaborate callback forms, induce a much-dreaded callback hell, a state of expressional rigor characterized by long chains of nested function applications. It is important to consider this when creating error resolution regimes centered on the use of callbacks—regimes that can be enhanced when employed in conjunction with some of the patterns discussed later in the chapter.

4.3 Default Values

A default value is a function parameter that is propagated as a return value when some condition other than that which characterizes its host function's core behavior, often a failure of some kind, is encountered on invocation. The term "fallback" has a high degree of synonymy with the concept of a default value, and is often used interchangeably with it, for it implies that whatever value is given the designation is used as some final recourse, when an expected value cannot be computed per some rule. In the following rewrite of the head function from the previous segment, the callback from earlier is replaced with an atomic value that is returned when the first list item in the first argument, indexed at 0, cannot be retrieved.

A binary head function that takes a default value as an argument

```php
function head(array|object $list, mixed $default = null): mixed
{
  return $head[0] ?? $default;
}
```

The variant shown above is significantly less verbose than the callback variants from earlier in the chapter. By assigning null to the default parameter, suitably named $default, on function creation, a subsequent invocation of the new version of the head function can be more terse, with only one parameter as a mandatory requirement. Using a default parameter in the manner depicted below works much in the same way as the second callback from the preceding segment, except without the function call.

Handling errors with a default value

```
var_dump(
  // example 1
  head(
    [
      'foo' => 'foo',
      'bar' => 12,
      'baz' => 3.3312,
    ],
  ),
  // example 2
  head([], 'undefined'), // returns "undefined"
);
```

Because any scalar value can count as a valid fallback, it helps, when writing functions in such a way as to return error-signifying values in place of exceptions, to represent failure states as data that readily communicate failure. Falsy values, data construable as the boolean false when evaluated in logical expressions by the PHP interpreter, have been used thus far because they satisfy this property. Fallbacks, however, for all the arbitrariness they enable, do not often convey any useful error information like an exception does, outside of a singular value that, on detection, would warrant special consideration. Overcoming this limitation without halting the runtime might require the use of an error message.

4.4 Error Messages

An error message is a notification that contains information that describes a failure. Like an exception, it allows for the elaboration of failure states and, thence, the inclusion of contextually explanatory phrases in error handling sections of programmatic flow control. Because an error message does not halt the runtime and, thus, the evaluation of any of the expressions that follow it by the interpreter, it requires that selective forwarding of error state as one of either a default value, a callback expression, or a non-modifiable, unparameterized descriptive value (also potentially falsy) should be enforced to prevent the potential (accidental) use of invalid data in valid expressions. Consider the division function below.

A divide function that triggers an error when a divisor of zero is passed to it

```php
function divide(int|float $dividend, int|float $divisor):
    int|float|null
{
  if ($divisor === 0) {
    \trigger_error("Cannot divide by zero");

    return null;
  }

  return $dividend / $divisor;
}
```

Passing the number zero as a divisor to the division function above, an action that would otherwise trigger a fatal error and thence terminate the script in which the faulty expression would reside, is accounted for in the function's signature. The said default runtime-halting behavior is averted by tandem use of a user warning, an error message triggered via the `trigger_error` function, and the falsy value null. The final result of any attempt to divide any dividend by zero, with the function shown above, is as follows.

Error message written to output device when division by zero is attempted

```
PHP Notice:  Cannot divide by zero in file.php on line 6
NULL
```

Because error messages like the one displayed above are persisted to an error stack of sorts by the PHP interpreter, handling them, that is, accounting for their potential occurrence in the expressions they might spawn from, via the use of specialized artifacts, provides an avenue for applying discretionary supplementary error expressions. By first prefixing a divide call with the symbol "@" to suppress the error message and thus prevent it from appearing in the output device, as shown in the most recent snippet, and then invoking `error_get_last` and `error_clear_last` to, respectively, retrieve the most recent error message on the error stack and pop it from the same structure, it is possible to achieve something similar to `try/catch` without ever bringing the execution of the host script to a standstill. Such behavior can be achieved as in the example below.

Retrieving the most recent division error upon attempting to divide by zero

```
$result = @divide(12, 0);

if ($err = \error_get_last()) {
  echo \sprintf(
    "Error: %s\nFile: %s\nLine: %s\n",
    $err['message'],
    $err['file'],
    $err['line'],
  );

  \error_clear_last();
}
```

Handling errors in the manner depicted above affords one access to descriptive information the language interpreter would otherwise print to the screen—an error message, the path to the file in which it was detected, and the line in the said file from which it originates. If there were ever to arise a need to persist such information to a store suited to housing its contents—a database of some sort, for instance—all the requisite logging expressions would have to, in a straightforward way, be worked into the specialized scope of such an error handling approach. Alternatively, if some homogenous, one-size-fits-all logging regime were deemed appropriate, the same error information, relayable via the callback passed to the native `set_error_handler` function, would have to be funneled into the same hypothetical arbitrary expressions, instead in the scope of a callback.

Though great for propagating contextual error information alongside usable error values, error messages are not the fixture in the PHP userland that exceptions are. Native language functions aside, there is little advertisement of error messages in the userspace. As such, there exists a need to confront exceptions head-on, without terminating host scripts, while ensuring that the functions prone to them remain composable.

4.5   Composable try/catch

The prevalence of exceptions in the PHP userspace cannot be understated. Because there is a really good chance of encountering them seeing as they are thrown by the language engine in the event of the occurrence of a fatal error, in several third-party libraries installable via Version Control Systems (VCSs) and, perhaps, in private, often proprietary subsystems authored in such a way as to tidy away artifacts usable in projects of the same designation, there exists a need to confront the possibility of encountering the runtime-halting behavior exceptions are synonymous with. PHP ships with a `try/catch` flow control feature that helps to this end. With `try/catch`, one can convert exceptions from a thrown state to one conducive to transit and inspection at rest—from a runtime staller to an object. Consider the example to follow.

A version of divide in which exceptions are converted to errors in a try/catch sequence

```
function divide(int|float $dividend, int|float $divisor):
    int|float|null
{
  $result = null;

  try {
    $result = $dividend / $divisor;
  } catch (Throwable $err) {
    \trigger_error($err->getMessage());
  }

  return $result;
}
```

In the above rewrite of the `divide` function from the previous segment, the default fatal error thrown by the PHP engine on detection of a divisor value of 0 is converted into a descriptive exception object and forwarded as a user notice. In this way, the runtime-stalling behavior of the fatal error/exception is averted; an appropriate message is thence propagated via an error message. While writing function signatures in anticipation of runtime-halting behavior, as in the most recent example, is certainly worthwhile, using a higher-order function into which a reusable `try/catch` flow sequence is tidied away is perhaps a better approach.

A higher-order function like bingo-functional's `toException` that takes an invocable function as its first argument and an arbitrary exception handling callback as its second offers the laziness discussed in the previous chapter as well as the runtime-stalling avoidance discussed thus far in this one. A replacement of the `try/catch` block with `toException` can be written as follows.

Replacing try/catch with a composable to Exception function

```
use function Chemem\Bingo\Functional\toException;

function divide(int|float $dividend, int|float $divisor):
    int|float
{
  return $dividend / $divisor;
}

$divide = toException(
```

```
  divide(...),
  function (Throwable $err): mixed {
    \trigger_error($err->getMessage());

    return null;
  },
);

$result = @$divide(12, 0);

// do something with the error value
```

In the new version of the runtime halting–avoidant division shown above, a new function, essentially a decorator of a simpler divide function that only contains a parameterized division operation, is created from the application of toException. The said decorator, on invocation with an errant divisor, funnels the resultant PHP fatal error into an error message, as in the previous example, and can be placed in a chain with other functions that are written in such a way as to be averse to throwing exceptions.

Facing exceptions head-on, with a higher-order function like the one depicted, helps neutralize their runtime-stalling behavior with function application. try/catch, a flow control artifact that is not inherently composable, is rendered so by a function to which success and error rules are passed on invocation. Making try/catch composable ensures that expressions dependent on native functions prone to fatal errors, third-party libraries, and other private tooling need only be appropriately decorated before being plugged into other expressions unburdened by exceptions. It allows for the use of explicit two-track error handling inherent to sum types—objects fit for the purpose of ensuring that compositions remain unbroken in the presence of errors.

4.6 Sum Types

Sum types are not a common recourse for error handling among PHP developers. Although their usefulness extends beyond error handling, they are especially equipped for it in PHP, for they are compatible with a pattern whose core emphasis is tracking successes and failures in expression chains. A sum type, also referred to as a union type, is simply a composite of distinct data structures that, at runtime, upon execution of a host expression, only evaluates to one of its constituents. It effectively represents a choice of an applicable data structure from a predefined, immutable set of options. PHP allows for the creation of arbitrary unions like the one in the example to follow.

A function the return type for which is a union of string and null types

```
function slugify(string $x, string $y): ?string
{
  if (\mb_strlen($x) < 3 || \mb_strlen($y) < 3) {
    return null;
  }

  return \sprintf('%s-%s', $x, $y);
}
```

Although the union that defines the expected return type options specific to the slugify function above passes the sum type "smell test," it fails to deliver any resilient error handling because its constituent types do not each have complementary functions defined on them to effect a composable flow control. The resilient error handling described here, and achievable with a sum type, assumes a two-track system of successes and failures, each with distinct function chains. Errors in such a system do not bring the runtime to a standstill, but rather evaluate to some isolatable error type. Such error handling, it must be said, works only in situations where the types in a union, the options from which to choose workable representations of success and failure, share a common API. The types null and string in the example are entirely scalar and markedly distinct and, while compatible with several userspace functions, do not share a unifying API. They are not true algebras.

Algebras

An algebra is simply a metastructure in which there resides a state, effectively a collection of relevant elements, and rules specifically governing the operations that can be performed on that state. An entity suited explicitly to the multiplication of natural numbers, for instance, can be considered an algebra wherein the said numbers are the elements of a specific set and the associativity underpinning the multiplication operation is representable in specific rules—functions that effect the said governing operation.

To effect patterns centered around the use of sum types, algebras should be constructed. In PHP, this precondition can be satisfied by using objects, which, as mentioned in a previous chapter, have a state that constitutes both data properties and (modificative) functions, or methods. It is with objects and the rules defined in them that success and failure states can be consistently encoded as algebras in a composite structure and handled via function application.

4.6.1 Maybe

Maybe is a sum type with which to represent desirable values in one path and discard all unwanted values altogether in another. It is a binary union wherein all usable data are propagated via a Just object and failures are represented as Nothing. Maybe is, by virtue of being the union of two algebras, an algebra itself and is typically encoded as such. It is, in PHP, where it is not provided out of the box as in Haskell or OCaml, written as a persistent class whose methods are differentially, polymorphically encoded in each of its constituents to reflect their respective differentiated handlings of successes and failures. Consider the following limited representation of a typically robust Maybe type.

A simple template for a Maybe algebra

```
readonly abstract class Maybe
{
  public static function just(mixed $value): Maybe
  {
    return new Just($value);
  }

  public static function nothing(mixed $value): Maybe
  {
    return new Nothing($value);
  }

  public abstract function map(callable $function): Maybe;
}
```

The class above is abstract and read-only to condition Maybe's extensibility and immutability. Maybe's sub-algebras, Just and Nothing, are, in the class anatomy above, operationalizable via static methods of the same respective names. Further still, the abstract quality of the map function defined on it ensures that differences in the Just and Nothing handlings of the data passed to them are deferred to the respective sub-algebras. This makes it such that the different interpretations of map are ultimately defined differently in the algebras that extend the Maybe type, per the rules regarding how they should each handle the data passed to them. An appropriate version of Just that extends the depicted Maybe algebra can be written as follows.

A simple template for Just, the first of two subtypes in the Maybe algebra

```
readonly class Just extends Maybe
{
  private mixed $value;

  public function __construct(mixed $value)
```

```php
    {
      $this->value = $value;
    }

    public function map(callable $function): Maybe
    {
      return new static(
        $function($this->value),
      );
    }
}
```

Because Just is the algebra in the Maybe union whose responsibility is propagating expressions deemed worthy of pursuing to a desired logical conclusion, to a point of finality where the rules fully encode the solutions to the problems they are modeled to solve, its makeup is such that any one of a broad set of values can be placed in its jurisdiction and assigned to its property named $value. Its constructor allows for the placement of an arbitrary value in its internal state, and the map function defined in it ensures that each application of a relevant, arbitrary function to its current state instantiates a new Just object, with a new expression.

Just is only one part of the Maybe union, however. The other part, Nothing, is effectively a sterile algebra, for it is assigned a null value that is non-modifiable, albeit, from an API perspective, generally compatible with Maybe. A simple encoding of Nothing that demonstrates its sterility is as follows.

A simple template for Nothing, the second of two subtypes in the Maybe algebra

```php
readonly class Nothing extends Maybe
{
    private mixed $value;

    public function __construct(mixed $value)
    {
      $this->value = null;
    }

    public function map(callable $function): Maybe
    {
      return $this;
    }
}
```

The sterility of the Nothing algebra means that it is intended to behave like a vacuum. Matter, the analog for data, does not exist in a vacuum. Likewise, data does not exist in the Nothing algebra. Subsumed in every Nothing object created from the class above is the primitive `null`, which, in PHP, perfectly represents the absence of a usable value. Every constructor call to the class shown above results in the placement of `null` inside an instantiated Nothing object. Furthermore, any attempt to modify any instance of the Nothing class depicted, via the map method defined on it, results in the propagation of the same object created on initial instantiation, as the algebra is, again, like a vacuum in which matter neither exists nor can be transformed, incapable of housing data and facilitating modifications to it. Nothing is, in this way, a programmatic dead end.

Maybe is usable in a variety of situations that call for the use of a binary algebraic union. A getter whose purpose is to extract a value from one of either an object or a hashtable that corresponds with a specified key can be written in such a way as to funnel a desired result—the outcome of a successful lookup—into a Just object and sterilize all failures in a Nothing object. Something like the following can prove demonstrative.

A function in which the success and failure of a lookup operation is mediated via a Maybe algebra

```php
use Chemem\Bingo\Functional\Functors\Monads\Maybe;

function pluck(array|object $list, int|string $key): Maybe
{
  return Maybe::fromValue(
    \is_object($list) ?
      $list->{$key} ?? null :
      $list[$key] ?? null,
  );
}
```

The getter shown above has a signature such that the branching expression that distinguishes a successful lookup from an unsuccessful one is funneled into the `fromValue` method. This function conditionally forwards a valid expression into a Just object or evaluates to a vacuum, Nothing, depending on whether the two arguments passed to it are the same. It eliminates the need to write separate instantiations of Just and Nothing in some sort of flow control structure, which, despite the aforedescribed convenience, is perfectly valid. As shown in the example below, the getter, upon invocation, produces an algebra with a unified, polymorphic API that can be interacted with in the same manner as the persistent objects described in Chapter 2.

Performing an erroneous lookup with the function that propagates a Maybe algebra

```
$key    = 9;
$result = pluck(
  \range(1, 5),
  $key,
)
  ->map(
    // square the number
    fn (int $value): int => \pow($value, 2),
  )
  ->map(
    $factorial = function (int|float $value) use
        (&$factorial): int|float {
      return $value < 2 ?
        1 :
        $value * $factorial($value - 1);
    },
  );
```

At the end of the chain of successive map calls shown above, Nothing is returned. The result of the chain is so because the invocation of **pluck** in the example above produces a vacuum as neither the index 9 nor a value slotted into the provided list at that index exists. Seeing as neither function applications nor real values are capable of existing in the vacuum that is Nothing, the function that squares the result of the getter and that which computes the factorial of the square are ignored. This result and the outputs of successful searches can both be further treated with secondary case analyses.

Case Analysis

Case analysis is a technique that focuses on evaluating all possible outcomes in a system through the application of functions. It is an application of pattern matching, a concept discussed in depth in a future chapter, and requires that, for each scenario, a relevant function be defined such that, when the interpreter, in computing the most appropriate of a set of evaluable options, selects a fitting option, its corresponding function expression is abstracted over whatever applicable state. Performing a case analysis on a sum type means applying a selection mechanism to a closed set of options—effectively all of its constituent algebras. Programmatically, any conditional flow control statement—a ternary, switch, if-else, and the like—could suffice in ensuring that only an expression deemed executable only when a particular algebra is encountered is indeed evaluated by the interpreter.

As far as the Maybe algebra is concerned, the case analysis implemented in its API is such that a default value is returned when a Nothing object is encountered and a function is applied to the value wrapped inside a Just object otherwise. Fittingly, the rule is abstracted into a function also named maybe, which, behavior-wise, unwraps Maybe objects in a manner that is congruent with similar implementations in languages where sum types like it are a mainstay. Something like the following should ensure that null is propagated to signal failure when it is encountered, like in the example from before, and that the eventual numerical result of the successive mathematical operations is retained in the event of a successful lookup.

Performing case analysis with the Maybe algebra

```
use function Chemem\Bingo\Functional\{
  Functors\Monads\Maybe\maybe,
  identity,
};

var_dump(
  maybe(
    null,
    identity(...),
    $result,
  ),
);
```

Irrespective of whether a fitting case analysis is applied or not, when used to handle errors, Maybe can feel rather limiting despite its validity. In behaving in such a way as to sterilize failures in a vacuum, Maybe conditions that the writer of expressions dependent on it forego the ability to use contextually workable non-null error values to enrich error reporting. It is prone to the same weakness as functions reliant on default values, and therefore, rules written so as to be reliant on it might not always effectively communicate defects and, thus, errors for which there might exist more descriptive information than a vacuum or default value can provide. For a richer error handling experience, a more comprehensive algebra, Either, can prove useful.

4.6.2 *Either*

Either's distinctive quality is its inherent support for more elaborate error types. With Either, it is possible to place an arbitrary error value in an object suited to handling failures, named Left, and propagate the result of a successfully evaluated expression in an algebra like Just from before, purposely designated as an object through which to forward successes, called Right. Either's Left algebra is not a total vacuum like its counterpart, but is still implemented as a sterile object whose contents are unmodifiable, upon instantiation, by the methods defined on it. Like

Maybe, the parent Either algebra can be written as an abstract, read-only class, a summarized version of which resembles the one featured below.

A simple template for an Either algebra

```
readonly abstract class Either
{
  public static function right(mixed $value): Either
  {
    return new Right($value);
  }

  public static function left(mixed $value): Either
  {
    return new Left($value);
  }

  public abstract function map(callable $function): Maybe;
}
```

The implementation shown above is not too dissimilar to that of Maybe from the previous section. As far as differences go, the only noteworthy changes are the names of the sub-algebras and thus paths through which to propagate successes and sterilize failures. Right, the designated success path in the Either scheme, is itself not too dissimilar to Just and can be written, per the specification of Either from which it inherits, like so.

A simple template for Right, the first of two subtypes in the Either algebra

```
readonly class Right extends Either
{
  private mixed $value;

  public function __construct(mixed $value)
  {
    $this->value = $value;
  }

  public function map(callable $function): Either
  {
    return new static(
      $function($this->value),
    );
  }
}
```

Right is synonymous with the word "correct," and its anatomy is such that expressions bound for the success path of a binary union, values placed inside of instances of it, are rendered modifiable via composition. Such behavior contrasts that of the Left algebra, whose sterility is bundled with the offer of discretion in choosing a descriptive error value. An appropriate Left class, which also inherits from the Either class featured earlier, can be written as follows.

A simple template for Left, the second of two subtypes in the Either algebra

```php
readonly class Left extends Either
{
  private mixed $value;

  public function __construct(mixed $value)
  {
    $this->value = $value;
  }

  public function map(callable $function): Either
  {
    return $this;
  }
}
```

Unlike Nothing, the Left algebra featured above is open to the placement of an arbitrary value in the resultant object's jurisdiction, on instantiation. But like Nothing, the said value, once encapsulated in a Left object, is rendered unchangeable by map and, in more elaborate versions of the algebra, other modificative methods as well.

Either can be used as a high-resolution replacement for Maybe. Its ability to facilitate a richer error propagation can be applied to the getter from before, whose signature can be repurposed to forward an elaborate error value instead of a vacuum. Something like the following can count as a valid reimagination of the pluck function from the previous segment.

A function in which the success and failure of a lookup operation is mediated via an Either algebra

```php
use Chemem\Bingo\Functional\Functors\Monads\Either;

function pluck(array|object $list, string|int $key): Either
{
  if (
    (\is_object($list) && !$result = $list->{$key} ?? null) ||
    (!$result = $list[$key] ?? null)
  ) {
    return Either::left(
```

```
      new Exception(
        \sprintf(
          'The key %s does not exist in the list',
          $key,
        ),
      ),
    );
  }

  return Either::right($result);
}
```

While there exists no function like `fromValue` in the bingo-functional Either API
to shorten the branching logic in the reimagined getter, the use of the algebra's right
and left methods in the manner depicted, in the respective success and error phases
of an if-else statement, perfectly captures the duality of the situation. In modeling
a propagable success path, the use of the Right algebra is similar to the use of Just
in the previous chapter segment. The use of the Left algebra, however, presents
the biggest difference. Emplaced in the constructor of the Left algebra used in the
reimagined getter is an exception, an object that, as earlier established, cannot stall
the runtime unless explicitly used in a throw expression. Although a simple string
could work, an exception that, at rest, offers access to causal high-resolution error
information can provide more descriptive value if a point of sterility—failure—is
reached.

Recreating the failure from before, with the result of an errant retrieval operation
funneled into the same chain of two successive mathematical operations, produces
an instance of the Left algebra. Encapsulated in the said instance is an exception
object bearing the message "The key 9 does not exist in the list." To unwrap the
resultant Either type, as in the previous segment with Maybe, a case analysis can be
performed as in the snippet below.

Performing case analysis with the Either algebra

```
use function Chemem\Bingo\Functional\{
  Functors\Monads\Either\either,
  identity,
};

$case = @either(
  // resolve Left algebra
  function (Throwable $err): mixed {
    \trigger_error($err->getMessage());

    return null;
  },
  // resolve Right algebra
  identity(...),
```

```
    $result,
);

// do something with error value here
```

For the Either algebra, the case analysis implemented, also in a function of the same name, is such that separate functions, one for each of the constituent types, Left and Right, are funneled as arguments alongside an instance of an object subject to evaluation. As in the Maybe case analysis example, the result of a successful lookup and further mathematical modification is retained via the identity function. Unlike the previous analysis, however, the error is treated a little differently: the error resolution pattern implemented in the section "Error messages" is effected in the Left-applicable callback above. When a lookup fails, the descriptive text in the exception object encapsulated in the Left algebra is funneled into an error message, and the value null is propagated to signify the absence of a value slotted into the provided list at the specified index.

Using Either in the manner depicted can be described as a tactful way of approximating the behavior of `try/catch` with a sum type in so much as simulating the throwing and subsequent catching of an exception is concerned. The throwing, in this case, is approximated by the construction of an error path with a fitting exception object, upon detection of a fault, whereas the catching is mimicked in the treatment of the error path in the first callback of the case analysis. While Either is an excellent choice for situations that warrant the retention of detail in success and failure paths, there exists yet another sum type suited to the same purpose with built-in exception object bindings that is becoming more commonplace in the PHP userspace—the promise.

4.6.3   *Promises*

The paradigm of asynchronous programming, that is, an approach to writing programs in which computations are interleaved in such a way as to keep the CPU busy and minimize the occurrences of idleness between successive executions, has gained a foothold in PHP. In the world of asynchronous programming, expressions are not always guaranteed to immediately produce a result on evaluation. In fact, expressions that initiate asynchronous actions often require that a pair of callbacks—one in which to propagate a success and the other into which to funnel a failure—be utilized to handle eventual outputs. Chaining callbacks, though viable, can negatively impact code readability and inflict tedium when handling long chains. To avoid such patterns in asynchronous code, special considerations should be made to ensure that outputs that may not be ready in time to be processed via any of the sum types described thus far can be treated in the same way as those emplaced in them—in a two-track algebraic system, the success and error paths of which are, respectively, open to composition and sterilization. Enter the promise—a sum type well suited to the said purpose.

Promises have two tracks, like the other algebras discussed in this chapter of the book—one for successes, known as a fulfillment path, and another for failures, referred to as a rejection path. The former works a lot like the Just and Right objects in the Maybe and Either algebras, respectively. The latter, however, exclusively propagates failures via exception objects. Failures are, in every implementation of the artifact, forwarded as throwable objects. To illustrate the two-track nature of the promise, a simple asynchronous HTTP request, as in the example below, can prove instructive.

> Installing react/http

The code in the snippet to follow can only work upon the installation of `react/http`, a package whose slate of contents includes artifacts required for making asynchronous HTTP client requests and spinning up asynchronous HTTP servers, as one would with a runtime like NodeJS. Installing the said package can be done with Composer, by keying an appropriate directive into a preferred console, like so.

Installing react/http via Composer

```
composer require react/http
```

Making an asynchronous HTTP request and processing the resultant response in a Promise

```
use React\Http\Browser;

$request = (new Browser())
  ->get(
    'https://jsonplaceholder.typicode.com/posts/110',
    [
      'content-type' => 'application/json; charset=utf-8',
    ],
  )
  ->then(
    function (ResponseInterface $response): void {
      echo \sprintf(
        "%s\n",
        $response
```

```
        ->getBody()
        ->getContents(),
    );
  },
  function (Throwable $err): void {
    echo \sprintf(
      "Error: %s\n",
      $err->getMessage(),
    );
  },
);
```

On display in the snippet above is an expression that utilizes React's HTTP client component, a class fittingly named `Browser`, whose methods, named after protocol verbs—GET, PUT, POST, and the like—each forward the eventual results of a different flavor of asynchronous HTTP client request and corresponding HTTP server responses into instances of a promise. Server responses associated with failure, those for which the status code is 400 or greater, are rejected, whereas everything else, particularly those in the 200–300 range of status codes, is fulfilled.

The featured expression is an instruction to retrieve the 110th post in the set of posts available on the Typicode website. It is a GET request that fails because no such record exists in the Typicode system. The eventual result of the asynchronous HTTP client socket relay, the "Not Found" (404) response sent by the Typicode server, bubbles up the function chain to the last function in it, where it is logged as a string prefixed with the label "Error."

As far as the promise that facilitates the composition and error handling in the example is concerned, it must be said that the method named "then" is critical to effecting any propagation of fulfillment and otherwise. It works like the map function defined in Maybe and Either contexts, but takes two arguments, the first of which is the callback applied on fulfillment and the second is the callback applied on rejection. By default, fulfillments and rejections are forwarded as they are, via the aforedescribed respective callbacks; however, they can each be converted to a contravening form—fulfillments to rejections and rejections to fulfillments—at the discretion of a programmer. A discussion of the means of converting fulfillments to rejections and vice versa lies outside of the scope of this book, but is worth noting nonetheless. Promises are great for writing two-track compositions, but are especially useful when deployed to add composition and error resolution to expressions whose results may not be readily available.

On that note, the comprehensive evaluation of alternatives to throwing exceptions, and therefore the fourth chapter of this book, is now complete. The next chapter investigates the theory that underpins the design of the algebras discussed in this one—Maybe, Either, and the promise—and offers a window into functors and monads, as well as algebraic techniques that further the composition agenda.

Chapter 5
Functors

5.1 Thinking in Terms of Functors

To round out the previous chapter were discussions of algebras—Maybe, Either, and the promise. The said algebras, despite subtle differences in the manner of sterilization of error values, all further the agenda of composition via a map operation—effectively an "apply-to-all" rule. The methods map and then, defined, respectively, on the former two algebras and the latter one, all perform the same role—that of a map operation similar to that discussed in Chapter 3. Because functors are containers that expose a map operation—an idea that is further elaborated on in this chapter—and the algebras discussed at the end of the preceding chapter fit the description, it is logically correct to assert that they are functors. This, the fifth chapter of the book, is dedicated to exploring the concept of the functor. Among the notable offerings of the chapter are discussions centered around embracing the algorithmic approaches inherent to functors, the logical system of Category Theory that operationalizes these approaches, and the applications of functors in everyday PHP code.

Movies, for example, can be considered maps if examined through a logical lens that seeks to connect the traits of the characters in them as well as the interactions the said characters have, with personhood and relational dynamics in the real world. By representing condensed but concise representations of interpersonal interactions, the scope of which could span moments, days, years, or even millennia, movies provide a connection between imitations, often the product of imagination, with distinct people and ideas in the real world. Not all characteristics in the human population need to be showcased in a movie, nor do all possible interactions between all human beings. For a movie to fulfill the role of an effective functor, it only needs to accurately depict believable interactions that fit the narrative into which they are woven and not every possible interaction or every possible distinct character for which there are, respectively, relations and human variety in the real world.

M. B. Lochemem, *Functional Programming in PHP*, https://doi.org/10.1007/979-8-8688-2468-5_5

When creating functors, which are maps of meaning that connect ideas, it is common to tidy away reusable parts of the sense-making process and apply those that can be used in more than one place severally. The former describes the use of abstraction, a concept that has been covered extensively thus far, while the latter speaks to the significance of generalization. When generalizing, the norm is to apply an abstraction independently and therefore reuse it **exclusively** in situations where it is applicable. As far as a movie is concerned, the characters featured in it, each with defining traits, are typically avatars for people in daily life. They are, like numbers in a number system that offer a means of counting in a particular base, an abstraction of ideas about people in real life. In progressing the plot to depict the same characters interacting with their environments and other characters in different ways, a movie is written in such a way as to generalize its characters in showcasing a range of behaviors and interactions no different from those that typify aspects of real life.

In computer programming, the connections formed via functors link constructs that can be described as sets comprising smaller sets (subsets) with very specific constituents: types and functions. The composition in each subset is such that, for each pair of types (manipulable entities like numbers, strings, objects, and the like), there exists a function that connects them. The source type primed for modification is, in each subset, connected to its target type produced on modification, via a (unary) function capable of performing the modification that links the two. Functors, in such a logical constellation of sets, act as meta-functions, the inputs for which are sets of one variety and the outputs are sets of another, input-related variety. The logical system that enables this approach in mathematics and software development is called Category Theory, which not only explains the technical origins of the functor but also, more importantly, provides the blueprint for creating meaningful mappings in code.

5.2 Category Theory

Category Theory is a mathematical subdiscipline concerned with abstract structures and the relationships between them. These abstract structures, called categories, resemble sets and are often considered as such. A category is, like a set, simply a collection of arbitrary items. Take, for instance, the categories depicted as circles in Figure 5.1.

Each circle represents a category, but not in great detail. Dissecting a single category, any one of the circles in Figure 5.1, reveals the set contents that make mappings between categories, the principle that operationalizes functors, possible. In each category are objects and the arrows that connect them. Figure 5.2 depicts this clearly.

The arrows between objects that effectively link them to each other are a proxy for transformative functions (or just functions) and are referred to as morphisms. Each morphism links a source object, from which it propagates, to a target object, to which it terminates and thereby describes a relationship.

Fig. 5.1 Diagrammatic
representation of categories

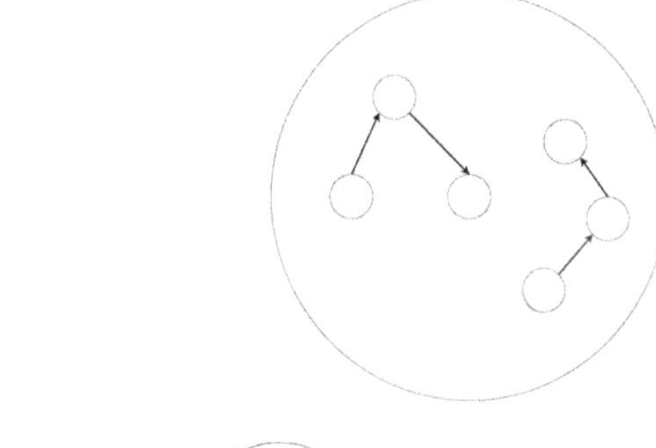

Fig. 5.2 Cross-sectional
representation of a category

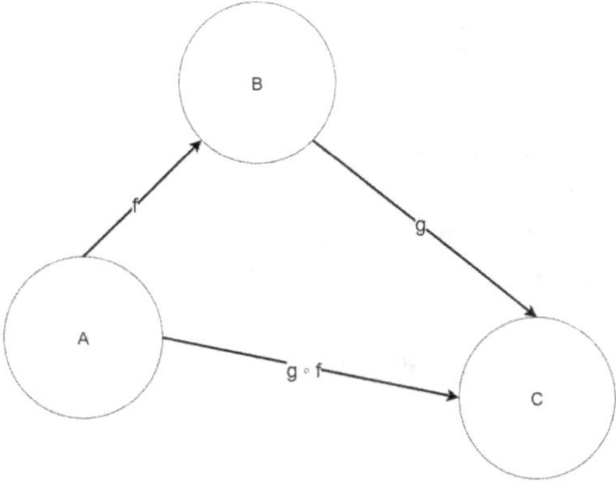

Fig. 5.3 Diagrammatic
depiction of a composition of
categories

5.2.1   Composition

Morphisms enforce the relationships between abstract structures in Category Theory. Their significance is such that they connect objects and, therefore, categories.
No object can exist without a morphism that links it to another in a system governed
by transformations from source to target. For every two morphisms in a connection
between three objects, there exists a third that summarizes the two consecutive
transformations involved in connecting the first to the third. This relationship is the
composition described in Chapter 3 only without the specific functions that apply
the mathematical identities featured in that part of the text. Consider Figure 5.3.

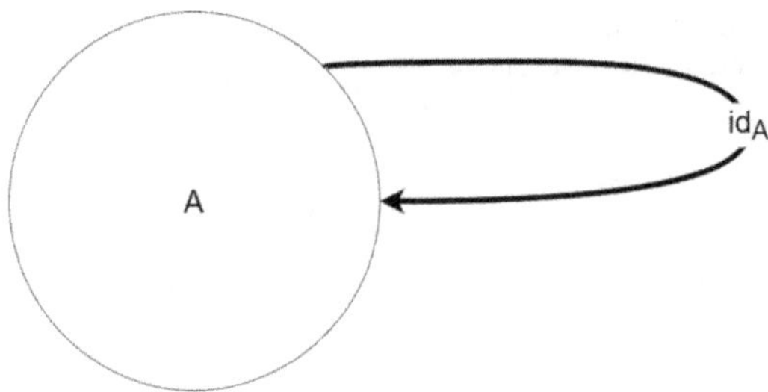

Fig. 5.4 Diagrammatic depiction of an identity morphism

In what can be considered an excerpt from Figure 5.2, the objects labeled A, B, and C describe a composition such that for the morphisms f and g, which, respectively, connect A to B and B to C, represented as the transformations $f : A \rightarrow B$ and $g : B \rightarrow C$, there exists a third morphism $g \circ f$ such that $g \circ f : A \rightarrow C$.

5.2.2 Identity

Much like the identity function seen in parts of the preceding text, there exists an identity morphism defined on each object in a category, an arrow directed toward itself. This unique morphism represents a possible transformation from an object to itself and is neutral to composition: each object retains its composability in spite of its presence. An identity morphism defined on the object A, for example, looks like Figure 5.4.

Identity, at a glance, might not seem impactful, but it can serve as a proxy for the meaningful operations that transform a source entity of one object into another entity classifiable as part of the same object. Think something like a string-to-string function or an integer-to-integer function.

5.2.3 Functors in Category Theory

Functors link categories. They are, in essence, morphisms that apply to entire sets whose constituents are objects and the morphisms that connect them. For this reason, it is valid to assert that functors are functions between categories that link the object and morphism mappings in a source category to those in a target category. Like the anatomy of an object, the anatomy of a functor can be represented diagrammatically, as depicted in Figure 5.5.

Shown above is a functor F that connects a category A to another category B. The state of the source category, A, in the mapping depicted is left unchanged by the application of the functor such that for every object and morphism defined inside of it, there exists a matching unique transformation in the target category,

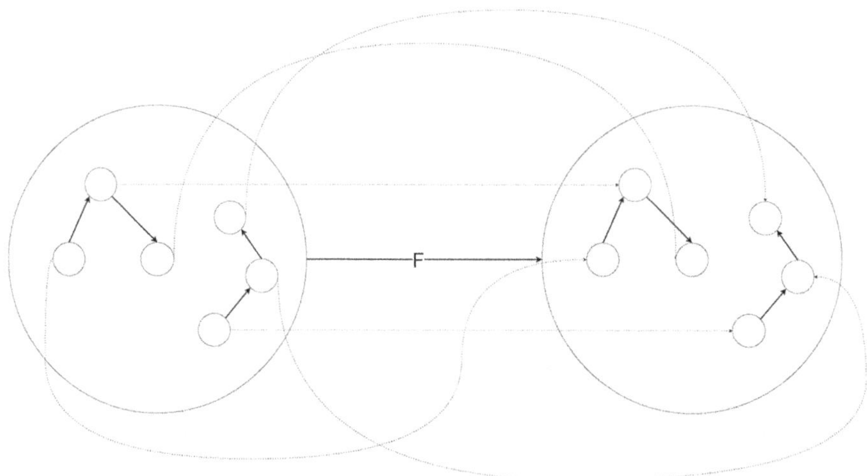

Fig. 5.5 Diagrammatic depiction of the Category Theory interpretation of a functor

B. As far as the movie example is concerned, the objects in A can function as a stand-in for people in the real world, for which there exist characters, portrayed by actors, in category B. Likewise, the interactions between people in the real world, representable as the morphisms in the source category, A, have a proxy in the movie realm, the morphisms in the target category, B.

5.3 Functors in PHP

Before making the jump to using functors in PHP, it makes sense to explicitly map out the equivalents of objects, morphisms, and categories in computer programming. Objects can be thought of and encoded in PHP as types—strings, floating-point numbers, booleans, and the like. Morphisms are the glue between types, the artifacts that, like the functors that approximate them, albeit in a magnified scope, connect them in such a way as to allow for transformations from one to another. Their equivalent in PHP (but really any language that satisfies the conditions for Functional Programming) are functions. Categories, the last of the trio of artifacts investigated in preceding segments, are algebras much like Maybe and Either from the end of the previous chapter: special entities capable of abstracting not only values of any one of several userspace types, but also the functions that can be applied to them.

Functors are useful in PHP, but really, any language in which they can be implemented, because they enable the use of generic functions to modify the data tidied into their jurisdiction. With a functor, a data unit as simple as a single string or as elaborate as a stream can be stowed away for the eventual application of fitting arbitrary rules that may or may not apply to situations beyond the one they are best suited to. Functors, in this way, obviate the need to explicitly derive functions with which to transform the data contained inside of them as well as any intermediate separate instances of the same data to accommodate the transformations performed on them. What this looks like in code is an algebra no different from those shown at the end of the previous chapter, a special kind of persistent object.

5.3.1 Functors Are Type Classes

Every implementation of a functor is a type class. Every functor is, therefore, a persistent class that supports operator overloading: one that contains methods whose implementations vary depending on the inputs they are provided. Operator overloading is commonplace in various programming languages, especially those with a rich templating system, like C++, that allow for some creative applications of operators to data they are (mostly) incompatible with. Regardless of the extent of its implementation in a target language, operator overloading is a practice undertaken with the aim of reusing a syntactic element, a symbol of some kind for which there is a corresponding computation triggerable on the application of fitting data (operands). It is syntactic sugar—a means of cajoling a translation program into accepting the generalization of a single operator.

The map method defined on functors is ripe for such overloading. By writing it in such a way as to apply to the internal state of the class in which it is defined, the function it accepts as its sole parameter, it can be primed for repeat use as a generic method such that each call to it produces a different result. This pattern, which was showcased in the demonstrations of the internals of the Just and Right algebras in the previous chapter, applies readily to a generic identity functor like the one below, whose introduction is befitting of this juncture in the book.

Identity Functor

```
readonly class Identity
{
  public function __construct(
    private mixed $value,
  ) {
  }

  public static function of(mixed $value): self
  {
    return new static($value);
  }

  public function map(callable $function): self
  {
```

```php
      return new static(
        $function($this->value),
      );
    }

    public function getValue(): mixed
    {
      return $this->value;
    }
}
```

With the functor above, it is possible to replicate the point-free behavior introduced in Chapter 3 via successive invocations of the map method. The process is rather simple. It starts with the placement of the data that would otherwise be passed to a "meta" unary function upon defining it with a utility like compose, in an instance of the functor via a constructor call. It proceeds with sequenced calls to map, with each call featuring a function placed at a desired point in an arbitrary chain before terminating in the extraction of a value produced at the end of the sequence of successive function applications. Intuitively, this process can be described as placing a value in an object and calling the same method defined on that object, map, severally. Consider the composition below.

A Point-Free Chain of Two Functions

```php
use function Chemem\Bingo\Functional\compose;

$ops = compose(
  // compute the cube here
  fn (int $val): int => \pow($val, 3),
  // convert the cube to a hex value
  \dechex(...),
);

var_dump(
  $ops(9), // prints "2d9"
);
```

In the featured chain are two functions, one that cubes a number and another that converts the cube value to its hexadecimal equivalent. The output of the former is funneled into the latter in the example by the meta-function created with the utility compose, which, in the same example, is applied to the integer 9 to produce a hex value of "2d9". With the identity functor introduced earlier in this segment, the same composition can be expressed with successive map calls, as follows.

Composition via Overloaded Map Method

```
$ops = Identity::of(9)
  ->map(
    fn (int $val): int => \pow($val, 3),
  )
  ->map(
    \dechex(...),
  );

var_dump($ops->getValue()); // prints "2d9"
```

Instead of passing the value 9 as an argument to a unary function, the said integer is first placed in a functor object in the rewrite above. The sequence of calls to map that follows retains the function order from the point-free example from before, with each call changing the meaning of the map method while modifying the value in the object to which its assigned callback is applied. The first call, that which applies the cube function to the functor's internal state, signifies an integer-to-integer mapping, whereas the second, an integer-to-hex conversion, represents an integer-to-string mapping. Being accommodative of these different meanings is, in essence, the enabler of the composition similar to that associated with the point-free style. This quality, referred to as ad hoc polymorphism, enables the multiple use of an overloaded map method to sequentially apply functions to an abstract state, producing a forward-chaining effect.

5.3.2   Functor Laws in PHP

For a type class to be considered a functor, it must satisfy the rules of identity and composition—ideas that are definitive fixtures in Category Theory. The two laws can be expressed as in Table 5.1.

Identity, discussed earlier in the chapter, is a law that dictates that identity morphisms in a source category be retained in a target category when a functor is applied to connect two categories. The schematic of the law, depicted in Figure 5.6, is such that, in mapping source to target, a functor links the identity morphisms in the source to those in the target category, in much the same way as it does the other source entities.

Table 5.1 Summary of functor laws

Law	Mathematical representation
Identity	$F(id) = id$
Composition	$F(g \circ f) = F(g) \circ F(f)$

F is a functor; g, id, and f are functions.

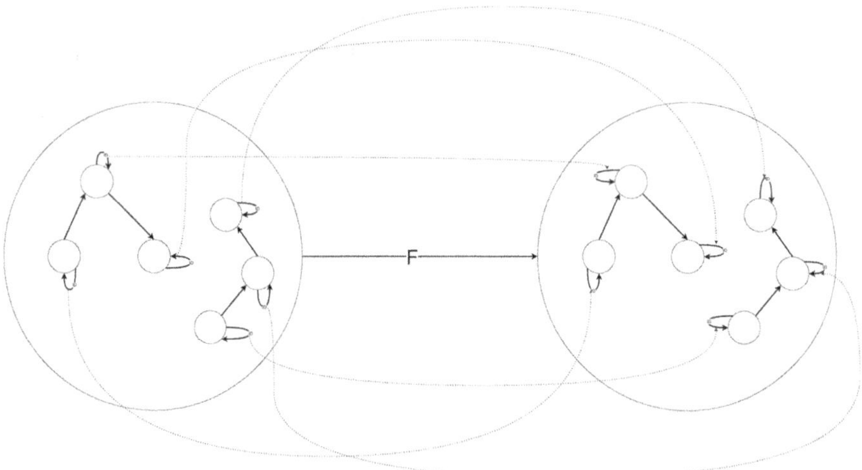

Fig. 5.6 Diagrammatic depiction of the identity law

In PHP, it is possible to prove the validity of the identity rule depicted above, with the type class defined earlier, by writing something like the following.

Proof of Validity of Identity Law

```
use function Chemem\Bingo\Functional\{
  equals,
  identity as id,
};

$F = Identity::of(9);

var_dump(
  equals(
    id($F),
    $F->map(
      id(...),
    ),
    true,
  ),
);
```

From the assertion above, it is not wrong to intuit that proving the identity law holds means checking that the identity function, the programming equivalent of the identity morphism, when applied directly to an instance of a functor produces the same result as mapping and thereby applying it to the value encapsulated in the same functor object.

Proving that the composition law, also discussed earlier, holds programmatically is a test of whether a function chain applied via map yields the same result as a sequence of map calls that feature the functions in the chain, in the same order. This proof was covered in the previous segment and can be succinctly summarized, as in the snippet below, with the same implements used earlier.

Proof of Validity of Composition Law

```
use function Chemem\Bingo\Functional\{
  compose,
  equals,
};

$f = fn (int $x): int => \pow($x, 3);
$g = fn (int $x): string => \dechex($x);

var_dump(
  equals(
    $F
      ->map($f)
      ->map($g),
    $F->map(
      compose($f, $g),
    ),
    true,
  ),
);
```

5.4 Monads

A monad is a special flavor of functor that makes it possible to map effects along with data. With a monad, the prospect of programming in such a way as to accommodate a context that may induce an impurity—an I/O call like reading from the Standard Input Device (STDIN) or an attempt to relay a datagram via a socket, for example—is reconciled with the principle of composition via type class. Monads, therefore, help confront everyday effect-inducing possibilities, "real-world" scenarios that often require that entire systems communicate with each other, typically via means whose scopes exceed those of simple functions like many of the ones written thus far. Essential to understanding the concept of the monad is the idea of the natural transformation, a foundational principle in Category Theory that informs attempts at programming with effects.

5.4.1 *Natural Transformations*

Already discussed are mappings between categories. Natural transformations describe relationships between functors. The catch here is that the condition of naturality must be upheld. Naturality is, in essence, a quality of morphisms being commutable. When an operation is described as commutable, a quality represented in the snippet below, it is described as being able to retain its result regardless of the order of its operands.

$$x + y + z = x + y + z \tag{5.1}$$

$$z + x + y = x + y + z \tag{5.2}$$

$$y + z + x = x + y + z \tag{5.3}$$

$$y + x + z = x + y + z \tag{5.4}$$

$$\cdots \tag{5.5}$$

The sum of three numbers, x, y, and z, can be represented in different ways—with the respective operands being shuffled to produce different sequences that all but evaluate to the same total. As far as mappings between functors go, natural transformations map morphisms in one functor to those in another. This mapping is such that, for each morphism in a source category, there exists a second morphism and, therefore, another pair of commutative objects in the target category. Please regard Figure 5.7.

The morphism Ff is a mapping of the source morphism f via the functor F, while the morphism Gf is a mapping of the same source morphism via another functor, G. For each object in the source category, there exists a mapping in the target category α that connects its F and G versions and thence forms a set, a square of sorts. For naturality to hold, the paths Ff to α and α to Gf should be the same

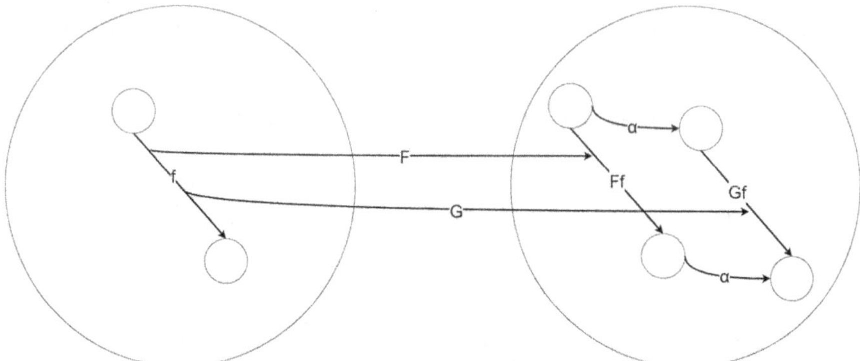

Fig. 5.7 Diagrammatic depiction of a natural transformation

and thence commute. What this means is that composing α and Ff and chaining α into Gf should yield the same result, irrespective of the starting point of each of the stated paths. It is possible to get from F to G and from G back to F because the paths Ff to α and α to Gf are the same. In this way, the following identities are valid.

$$\alpha \circ F(f) = \alpha \circ G(f) \tag{5.6}$$

$$F(f) \circ \alpha = G(f) \circ \alpha \tag{5.7}$$

To make this relationship easier to understand, imagine f as a function whose input is a string and output is an integer—a mapping from integer to string that can be represented as $f : Integer \rightarrow String$. F would, in this hypothetical setup, as per standard functor behavior, map f and the objects it connects to entities in a target category, to the effect of taking on the form $Ff : FInteger \rightarrow FString$. G, the newest entrant in this segment, would also, like F, map f, integer, and string types to the entities in the same category and thus take on the form $Gf : GInteger \rightarrow GString$, but only in the presence of α, a "bridge" function that connects G to F, but really $GInteger$ and $FInteger$ as well as $GString$ and $FString$. The precondition for naturality is the presence of α, a polymorphic function, which, in linking two variants of input and output types, makes it possible to map one variant, in this case, of a string in F, to a final form, a variant of an integer in G, in the same category.

Programmatically, placing a value in a functor via a call to the method `of`, as shown in the previous examples, achieves one natural transformation, the F part of Figure 5.7. The operation called *return* in most pure functional languages invokes a class constructor and returns a new functor object. To complete the commutative naturality and thus create a monad from the functor, an implementation of G would have to be added. Implementing G per the aforediscussed naturality rules would mean creating a separate method that, like `map`, also returns an instance of the same functor, but ultimately serves as a proxy for the polymorphic function α. This function, called `bind` in most functional syntaxes, allows for the application of a function that transforms a value encapsulated in the functor it is defined on, propagating its result in a new instance of the same functor—essentially the mapping represented by G in Figure 5.7. The `bind` method can be written as follows.

Bind Operation Defined on a Functor

```php
public function bind(callable $function): self
{
   return $function($this->value);
}
```

It is worth stating that the presence of α is implied in the implementation above. The starting point of any bind operation is, like that of a map, the value in the functor—Fa, where a is an object that represents any workable data. The first form of α retains this data, funneling it into the state Ga. Its point of termination, where it returns, is the endpoint of the second form of α, the state Gb. The bind operation, therefore, performs a map operation but only on functions whose return values are functors. From a Category Theory perspective, it creates two forms of any function that can be passed to it: the first, like map, which transforms a into b in a functor, and the second, which transforms a into a functor-encapsulated version of b in the same environment. In factoring naturality, it is possible to arrive at an improved definition of a monad. A monad is a functor that has two natural transformations defined on it: return, responsible for placing a value inside of its jurisdiction, and bind, responsible for applying a function that returns a separate instance of the same functor.

5.4.2 Monads and Effects

The point of using a monad is to overcome a mechanical limitation in functions whose inputs comprise simple types like integers and boolean values and outputs consist of similar primitives. Such functions, when viewed exclusively through the lens of purity discussed in Chapter 2, allow little room for the application of computational context. This context is essentially any metadata and actions that can induce impurities in function signatures and violate referential transparency. In, first, abstracting any usable state and, second, placing the relationships that exist between simple types in functions that can be applied to that state, functors are readied for the application of polymorphic functions, which complete a naturality order and allow for such context to be inserted into them without ever leaking to an external environment. If, for instance, a stream is created in reading data via a network request in a monad designed for network I/O so as to be able to propagate a server response as a string, the setup of the socket and potentially any errors, significant or incidental to either success or failure in the stream **sans string output**, can be contained in the monad without altering the signature of a function that uses it.

5.4.3 Monad Laws in PHP

Monads adhere to special laws that center around the use of the methods return and bind, all introduced in previous segments. The laws, summarized in Table 5.2, are proofs of a monad's ability to connect data structures flexibly.

The first law, left identity, is simply a check for the ability of a call to the bind function on an algebra in which a value x resides, with an arbitrary function f, to return the same result as a direct application of the same function f to the same value x. The proof of this law, which can be thought of as a test of the return function's ability to compose with a bind operation, can be written in PHP with an updated functor like so.

Table 5.2 Summary of monad laws

Law	Mathematical representation
Left identity	$return\ x >>= f = f \circ x$
Right identity	$m >>= return = m$
Associativity	$(m >>= f) >>= g = m >>= (x \to f(x) >>= g)$

m is a monad. f and g are functions. x is a value encapsulated in a monadic context. $>>=$ is a bind operation. $return$ is a monad constructor.

Proof of Validity of Left Identity Law

```
use function Chemem\Bingo\Functional\equals;

$f = fn (int $val): Identity =>
  Identity::of(
    \pow($val, 3),
  );
$x = 9;
$m = Identity::of($x);

var_dump(
  equals(
    $m->bind($f),
    $cube($x),
    true,
  ),
);
```

The second law, right identity, is yet another test of the composability of return and bind. It states that the bind method defined on a monad, when invoked with a call to the return method also defined on it, should return the same monad—an instance of the type class containing the same value. The proof of this can be written as follows.

Proof of Validity of Right Identity Law

```
var_dump(
  equals(
    $m,
    $m->bind(Identity::of(...)),
    true,
  ),
);
```

Finally, the associativity law is perhaps the most straightforward assertion of the composability of bind. It states that chaining two functions, f and g, with bind produces the same result as passing a composition of f and g to a bind operation defined on the same monad. The implication of this law is the same as that of the functor law of composition described earlier and highlights the applicability of the principle of associativity defined in Chapter 3: sub-chains that can each be factored into a larger chain can be formed with slightly stylistically variegated calls to bind. In PHP, the following can suffice.

Proof of Validity of Associativity Law

```
$g = fn (int $val): Identity =>
  Identity::of(
    \dechex($val),
  );

var_dump(
  equals(
    $m
      ->bind($f)
      ->bind($g),
    $m->bind(
      fn (int $val): Identity => $x($val)->bind($g),
    ),
    true,
  ),
);
```

Monad laws, in addition to informing the predictable, flexible behavior of monads, ultimately demonstrate that chains of regular functions with no monadic context, that take and return commonplace data types, can be retained in a monadic environment and used with methods like bind and map to tactfully modify data encased in monadic structures. Simply put, the manner in which generic functions are chained with bind does not matter, provided the propagation of types via bind (and map) occurs in lockstep with an intended arbitrary sequence.

5.5 Practical Monads

The identity functor discussed thus far is a generic monad that can prove useful in contexts that call for its application, but perhaps might be best sidelined in favor of algebras with much the same makeup built to address specific problems in which a particular type of side effect is inherent, in situations where there is potential for the specific side effect to manifest. From handling everyday I/O involving reading from files and writing to them to delicately managing program states in monadic environments, the monads in the list to follow provide useful strategies for sanitizing several kinds of effects that would otherwise undermine the purity of simple functions.

5.5.1 The I/O Monad

Most useful programs perform at least one Input/Output (I/O) operation. The problem with I/O, as discussed already, is that many such operations are impure. The proneness of I/O operations to modifying data, both native and foreign to the programs they are part of, warrants consideration of a special algebra into which to diffuse I/O effects. Enter the I/O monad—a solution to I/O-related woes. Writing I/O-effecting functions in such a way as to return an instance of the I/O monad makes it possible to funnel potentially volatile I/O operations—a filesystem interaction or system process, for instance—into a monadic environment from which their end result, typically simple userland primitives, can be extracted. Intuitively, the I/O monad provides a means to hide effectful I/O operations while ensuring that the functions in which they are defined return an I/O object and not a different result for every set of inputs they receive. Take a look at the sanitized file read operation below.

Sanitized file read with the I/O monad

```
use Chemem\Bingo\Functional\Functors\Monads\IO;

$unsafe = IO::of(
    function (): string {
        $fd      = \fopen('file.txt', 'r');
        $data    = '';

        while ($contents = \fgets($fd)) {
            $data .= $contents;
        }

        \fclose($fd);

        return $data;
    },
);

echo $unsafe
    ->bind(
        fn (string $contents): IO =>
            IO::of(
                fn (): string => \strtoupper($contents),
            ),
    )
    ->exec();
```

The text contents of the file named "file.txt" are streamed into memory in an unsafe, impure operation before they are converted to their uppercase equivalents in the monadic composition above. Calling **exec** unwraps the I/O monad in which the unsafe file read and character case modifications are performed, extracting the uppercase string produced as a result of combining them. This unwrapping can be deferred, and is therefore lazy, much like the mechanisms baked into each of the specialized monads to follow. When in doubt, wrap any unsafe operation in the I/O monad.

5.5.2   The Reader Monad

Managing configuration data across multiple functions is the calling card of the reader monad. Configuration data here refers to any unit of information that can be used to operationalize a more elaborate operation. Objects that can be injected as dependencies into others, as in programs that utilize dependency injection, and a list of entries in a file containing workable settings—user-defined variables in a .env file, console application preferences stored in a .yml file, and whatnot—for example, fit the mold of data that can be shuttled across functions applied in a reader environment. Please turn your attention to the demonstration below.

Reader Monad in Action

```
use Chemem\Bingo\Functional\Functors\Monads\Reader;
use function Chemem\Bingo\Functional\Functors\Monads\bind;

$env = bind(
  fn (string $user): Reader =>
    Reader::of(
      fn (array $env): string =>
        \sprintf(
          'Hello, %s. This script resides in the directory %s',
          $user,
          $env['PWD'],
        ),
    ),
  Reader::of(
    fn (array $env): string => $env['USER'],
  ),
);

var_dump(
  $env->run(
    \getenv(),
  ),
);
```

Defined in the reader monad environment above are a function that extracts the "USER" value, effectively the system username, from the data in its jurisdiction, its configuration data, and another that combines the username with another value in the same configuration, the present working directory, accessible via the key "PWD," into a message that reads "Hello, <USER>. This script resides in the directory <PWD>." Until the configuration, a list of system variables encoded as an array, is explicitly passed to the reader via the `run` method, the reader monad assigned to the variable `$env` remains in an unresolved state—a chain of monadic functions awaiting a fitting parameter. Because of this, the reader monad behaves lazily and can therefore be used creatively to the extent of chaining multiple getters to produce a single result, in this case the aforestated message, from the same configuration artifact.

5.5.3 *The State Monad*

Shared global state is difficult to manage in a language like PHP due to the high likelihood that its composition will include mutable data, which, as discussed in Chapter 3, can negatively impact function purity. The motivation for using the state monad is to minimize the occurrence of mutable global state and all its externalities by shunting data that would otherwise constitute it from function to function in a network of pure functions. It works a bit like the fold operation, also discussed in Chapter 3, as it stores an initial state, which is passed to it on instantiation, and a current state that is modified with each successful map operation performed via bind or one of its proxies. A state monad can be used to build a simple state machine like the one in the snippet below.

Simple State Machine Modeled into State Monad

```php
use Chemem\Bingo\Functional\Functors\Monads\State;
use function Chemem\Bingo\Functional\{
  Functors\Monads\State\gets,
  Functors\Monads\State\evalState,
  fold,
};

function playGame(string $input): State
{
  return gets(
    fn (array $state): array =>
      fold(
        function (array $acc, string $char): array {
          if ($char === 'a') {
            $acc = [
              ...$acc,
              'on'  => true,
```

```
          'val' => ($acc['val'] ?? 0) + 1,
        ];

          return $acc;
        }

        if ($char === 'b') {
          $acc = [
            ...$acc,
            'on'  => true,
            'val' => ($acc['val'] ?? 0) - 1,
          ];

          return $acc;
        }

        if ($char === 'c') {
          $acc = [
            ...$acc,
            'on' => false,
          ];

          return $acc;
        }

        $acc = [
          ...$acc,
          'on' => true,
        ];

        return $acc;
      },
      \str_split($input),
      $state,
    ),
  );
}

var_dump(
  evalState(
    playGame('abcaaacbbcabbab'),
    null,
  )(
    [
      'on'  => false,
      'val' => 0,
    ],
  ),
);
```

Abstracted into the function named playGame featured above is a projection, a special function that connects a set to an instance of itself. With the state monad,

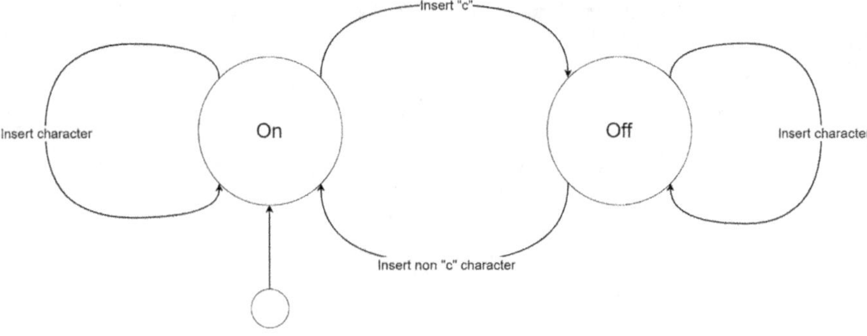

Fig. 5.8 Diagrammatic depiction of switch device state machine

projections like the one featured are used to transform an initial state and thence create a new, overwritable current state. The finite state machine modeled into the design of `playGame` is based on a simple device with a single switch and a counter whose overall mechanics are similar to those of a health bar in an action game, for instance. Diagrammatically, this state machine appears like Figure 5.8.

The two states of the switch, "on" and "off," are, respectively, encoded as true and false and accessible via the hashtable key "on." Transitions between the said states only occur when a character is entered into the device. If the character "a" is keyed into the machine, its counter, encoded as "val" in the same hashtable, is incremented, and the device's state is set to "on." Keying the character "b" into the same machine decrements its counter but also sets its state to "on." Inserting any lexeme other than "c," like the previous two cases, transitions the machine's switch state to "on," but leaves its counter untouched. Entering "c," however, triggers a transition to an "off" state without modifying the device's counter.

Going back to the snippet, the projection responsible for effecting the transition is a simple fold operation applied to the character sequence passed to the `playGame` function. It is placed in the monadic environment of a state monad by the function "gets" and thus primed for lazy evaluation via the function `evalState` that internally calls the monad's `run` method and unwraps its result, revealing both the current (new) state and the initial one from which it is derived. Passing the sequence "abcaaacbbcabbab" to the `playGame` function results in a switch in an "on" state and a counter whose value is zero—a value that, in a more elaborate action game system, might signify full health bar depletion.

> State vs. Reader

It can be argued that the state and reader monads can be used interchangeably because of their attunement to holding state, and there are likely several scenarios that can vindicate this line of thought. It is, however, important to remember that the two monads are distinct, irrespective of any potential overlaps. The state monad is best suited to situations characterized by a need to retain an initial state and another to produce a new state from it with each projection. The reader monad, on the other hand, works best when used to create a somewhat heliocentric system whose center is a singular environment state that is orbited by arbitrary projections.

5.5.4   *The Writer Monad*

Chaining bind or map calls with a writer monad often means creating a trail of descriptive information similar to the data in a log. The monad produces, in addition to values computed via its map and bind operations, usable "side" data of any arbitrary type. The usefulness of this logging is threefold: with a writer monad, it is possible to construct a log, albeit in memory, track state modifications via carefully written projections, and even recompute previous states, if a recipe for recombination, inclusive of relevant log data and appropriate functions, is made available. Generally, the writer monad is the logging functor. Shown below is a simple logger whose design is such that the annotative descriptions of the operations they feature alongside of are persisted to a writer monad's internal registry.

Writer Monad in Action

```php
use Chemem\Bingo\Functional\Functors\Monads\Writer;
use function Chemem\Bingo\Functional\Functors\Monads\Writer\{
logger,
execWriter,
writer,
};

$logger = fn (): Writer =>
  writer(5, 'put 5')
    ->bind(
      fn (int $val): Writer =>
        writer(0, 'add 2')
          ->map(
            fn (int $result): int => $result + ($val + 2),
          ),
    );

var_dump(
  execWriter(
    $logger(),
  ),
);
```

In the snippet above, the messages "put 5" and "add 2," which describe two operations performed in succession, the first a "return" operation involving the integer 5 and the second an addition of the integer 2 applied via `bind`, are placed in the monad's jurisdiction. A subsequent call to the function `execWriter` in the same example extracts only the registry whose contents are the aforedescribed messages. While the above showcase of the writer monad's registry might not have much real-world value, as there exist more robust options for persisting loggable information, such as file or database streams that are still functionally integrable, the registry in the writer monad, because of its openness to several types of data, can be used in a history-dependent event sourcing setup. Event sourcing is an approach to building distributed systems that prioritizes storing all loggable information about the state transformations that occur in them, in the exact sequence of occurrence. While event sourcing is not within the scope of this book, an excellent article titled "Event Sourcing with the Writer Monad" could serve as a nice supplement to the material in this segment.

5.5.5   *The List Monad*

Concluding the list of most noteworthy real-world monads is the list monad, which, as its name suggests, produces list data, usually of a nondeterministic kind. The implication of this is that a single application of the list monad can produce several outputs, conveyed in a list, from a single input. Projecting the total number of male rabbits born in each generation for three generations is a nondeterministic idea that can be encoded with the list monad. Consider the example to follow.

Simple Nondeterministic Model of Male Rabbit Births

```
use Chemem\Bingo\Functional\Functors\Monads\ListMonad;
use function Chemem\Bingo\Functional\{
  Functors\Monads\ListMonad\fromValue,
  constantFunction,
};

$replicate  = fn (int $count, string $value): ListMonad =>
  fromValue(
    \array_fill(0, $count, $value),
  );

$generation = constantFunction($replicate(3, 'male'));

$result     = fromValue(['parent'])
  ->bind($generation)
  ->bind($generation)
  ->extract();

var_dump($result);
```

Assuming a litter size of six babies and an even sex ratio of 1 : 1—one male rabbit for every female conceived—the number of males born can be encoded as a constant function, the output of which is an array with identical entries named "male." In the example above, one such encoding is combined with a list monad to produce a list of male children with nine entries, three per generation, in three generations that originate from a parent. Internally, the list monad concatenates the previous output with the next and then flattens the result to the effect of producing a combination of outputs from a single input set. Please consider using it to model series such as the simple one depicted above.

This, the fifth chapter of the book, is now complete. The functors and monads discussed here function like an insulating rubber sheath that protects electricity cables from environmental damage and shields users from electric shocks. Following this train of thought, the data tidied away in functors act as a proxy for the electricity cables; the functions applied to the data are the analog for the electricity transmitted via the cables; the side effects, absorbed into the functors on application of the vectors that transmit them, are the hazards that necessitate insulation. The next chapter explores how all the concepts discussed thus far factor into the design of systems built with concurrency aforethought.

Chapter 6
Functional Programming and Concurrency

6.1 PHP's Capabilities

As stated clearly in the introduction, PHP was conceived as a templating language: a derivative of the C programming language. Because of PHP's transitive relationship with the low-level APIs that enable the concurrent execution of programs, its userspace is tunable so as to avail PHP users of concurrency primitives that are rather commonplace in C. There is a catch, however. The Zend engine, the foremost distribution of the language's interpreter, is architected in such a way as to prioritize handling requests without retaining any residue, in a single thread. All concurrency utilities ported over to the PHP language from C, therefore, in being deemed usable in the language userspace, neither cannibalize this model nor flat-out contradict it. The rest of the discussion on concurrency and how it relates to Functional Programming is informed by an understanding of the options compatible with the paradigm and accessible in the userspace, which are as follows.

1. **Multithreading**: An option that is best suited to versions of the language interpreter that are considered thread-safe, multithreading is an approach whose emphasis is on splitting work, synonymous with a processing load or simply data, among multiple, combinable dispatchable units. For multithreading to succeed, great care should be taken to ensure that re-entrant functions, those that can be run several times, paused, and restarted, without haphazardly impacting a global state, are dispatched. Pure functions are re-entrant as they satisfy all the aforelisted criteria, but are also a great fit because of their predictability, a quality forfeited in bad designs.

2. **Multiprocessing**: Like multithreading, multiprocessing is an approach that often requires that work be divvied up, only, this time, among sub (or child) processes, effectively instances of running applications that spawn from a single caller.

M. B. Lochemem, *Functional Programming in PHP*, https://doi.org/10.1007/979-8-8688-2468-5_6

Processes are a viable option when building atop Operating Systems that have a monolithic, hierarchical structure and can be used in much the same way as threads, only with different kernel-based synchronization controls. Because processes are kernel residents, extra effort need be put in to prevent errors at the OS level.

3. **Evented I/O**: Popularized by NodeJS, the evented I/O model is one that best suits single-threaded runtimes like PHP. It seeks to reduce CPU idleness between sequential executions and effects a regime of interleaved I/O in a single dispatcher called an event loop that listens for changes to file descriptors and effects the arbitrary actions defined as performable on each such change. Unknown to many PHP developers is the language's out-of-the-box support for this concurrency-enabling technique and the options available for enhancing what exists in the userspace. Evented I/O is compatible with promises like those discussed at the end of Chapter 4, for its execution model makes it such that results of expressions, the data (or work) otherwise dispatchable via a thread or process, may not materialize in the exact moment when the expressions that produce them are executed.

> Zend Thread Safety

Builds with Zend Thread Safety (ZTS) are imperative for the code in the following sections to work properly. Thread safety is a technique that can be worked into low-level code to guard against the threat of corruption of its mutable global state by simultaneously executing threads. Built into every thread-safe version of PHP is a protective safety layer that enables execution of the language runtime in hyper-threaded environments. If you have used one of either Apache to serve PHP code on Windows or the Fast Process Module (FPM), you have likely enjoyed the protections offered by thread-safe builds of PHP, as the said software is built expressly for maximizing throughput in PHP processes by running them inside threads. To check whether your current installation is ZTS-enabled, type the following in a console of your choosing.

Checking for PHP Version

```
$ php --version
```

If the parenthesized label that reads "(ZTS)" is missing from the output of the above directive, proceed to compile a version of PHP with the `-|enable-maintainer-zts` flag, if your preference is to build PHP from source or download a ZTS version from the downloads section of the PHP website.

6.2 Multithreading in PHP

The rationale for using threads with the express purpose of increasing application throughput has, like many things explored in the book thus far, a real-world parallel. Project managers, in their capacity as administrators, have the ability to multiply assign and schedule tasks for each project they are tasked with overseeing. In doing so, they fulfill a role analogous to that of a calling process, from which threads can be spawned to much the same effect—fast-tracking attainment of some kind of target. Multithreading is a means of parallelizing computations with multiple dispatchable units, threads, while sharing process resources. Threads, like the tasks in a project schedule, are defined in a parent context—a calling process in this case. Each thread is a lightweight entity that has unique stack and register values, but only a share of the calling process's memory allotment. To use such units in a multithreading scheme means combining their (often) disparate results into a shared context—that of the caller—and thus synchronizing them. Such synchronization, due to the residency of threads in userspace, occurs with minimal scheduling overhead but is prone to race conditions and the data races that result from them. In PHP, there exist two approaches to multithreading with shared fundamentals, but different approaches to synchronization. Each philosophy is embodied by an extension authored by the same developer, Joe Watkins, for thread-safe (ZTS) versions of the PHP interpreter. The first, ext-pthreads, signifies a share-nothing approach to multithreading, whereas the second, ext-parallel, embodies a more elaborate, parallel and sequential composition-friendly, Communicating Sequential Processes (CSP) philosophy. Pure functions, in their many forms, and the techniques they are interoperable with, apply to both philosophies regardless of their differences, for they are not only re-entrant, but also easy to reason about.

6.2.1 Share Nothing with ext-pthreads

Developed as a direct port of the POSIX threads (pthreads) library, ext-pthreads is an extension for PHP 7 designed specifically for multithreading. Internally, it operates by duplicating instances of the PHP interpreter in each thread and enabling the parallel execution of PHP code. ext-pthread's "share nothing" philosophy mirrors standard PHP's in this way, as each thread is treated, like every request sent to a PHP server, in isolation, with extra guardrails to prevent haphazard modification of PHP data by multiple parallelly executing units. The guardrails architected into the extension are storage tables that prevent data corruption by locking data on each read and write operation. Per this setup, if two simultaneously executing contexts, one that, say, appends a string "bar" to a string "foo" and another that appends a string "qux" to the same string "foo," were encoded in a pthreads-powered system, the value "foo" would be written to the special storage area, the storage table, and retained as is for the former read and append operation and similarly for the latter modification.

From an API perspective, pthreads ships with a simple extensible Thread class, complete with an interpreter context, in essence, a clone of the PHP interpreter that allows for siloed translation of executable userspace code, accessible via instantiation of a child class, and a function through which to configure the entry of such code into the thread context, its run method. It is possible, with this knowledge, to implement a simple thread template from which to execute a variety of functions, in parallel, each in a separate thread, like in the example to follow.

pthreads Function Execution Template

```php
use function Chemem\Bingo\Functional\Functors\Monads\IO\IO;

class ExecFunc extends Thread
{
  private $func;
  private $params;
  private $result;
  private $joined;

  public function __construct(callable $func, ...$params)
  {
    $this->func   = $func;
    $this->params = $params;
    $this->result = null;
    $this->joined = false;
  }

  public function run()
  {
    $this->result = ($this->func)(...$this->params);
  }

  public static function call(callable $func, ...$params)
  {
    $thread = new static($func, ...$params);

    if ($thread->start()) {
      return $thread;
    }
  }

  public function merge()
  {
    return IO(
      function () {
        if ($this->joined) {
          $this->joined = true;
          $this->join();
```

```
        }

        return $this->result;
      },
    );
  }
}
```

The template above, called ExecFunc, inherits the thread context defined in the Thread class it is an extension of. Defined in its run method as a unit of work to parallelize is a single expression, the result of a call to the function passed to its constructor with its appropriate arguments, also passed to the same constructor, which is assigned to the property $result. The method call simply instantiates the thread context in which to execute the expression and starts the parallel execution, while the non-static merge function encases the synchronization of the thread and, thus, the merging of the result it computes into the main process from which it is spawned, in an instance of a lazily evaluable I/O monad. With the blueprint now established, it is possible to attempt to parallelize some seemingly expensive I/O operations. Kindly regard the snippet below.

pthreads Function Execution Template

```
use function Chemem\Bingo\Functional\{
  extend,
  partial,
};

use const Chemem\Bingo\Functional\concat;

$urigen   = partial(
  concat,
  '/',
  'https://jsonplaceholder.typicode.com',
  'posts',
  '1',
);

$post      = ExecFunc::call(
  '\file_get_contents',
  $urigen(),
)
  ->merge();

$comments = ExecFunc::call(
  '\file_get_contents',
  $urigen('comments'),
)
  ->merge();
```

```
$result   = $post->bind(
  function (string $post) use ($comments) {
    $decode = partial(
      '\json_decode',
      true,
    );

    return $comments->map(
      fn (string $comments): array =>
        extend(
          $decode($post),
          ['comments' => $decode($comments)],
        ),
    );
  },
);

var_dump(
  $result->exec(),
);
```

The execution template defined earlier is used in the example above to simultaneously retrieve a post and its comments, almost like one would when building something like a blog app. Partial application makes an appearance in the featured snippet and is used twice, first, to create a URL template for each of the aforementioned requests and, second, to prime the native JSON decoder to return a hashtable for all ensuing attempts at decoding server responses. Each of the results of the aforementioned requests, the post with an identifier of 1 and its comments, is funneled into an I/O monad upon successful parallelization and then combined into a single hashtable with a "comments" key created as a designated slot for the latter's contents.

ext-pthreads heralded an exciting approach to increasing the speed of PHP applications, but was discontinued by its creator. Concerned by the incompatibility of pthreads' internals with what, at the time, were those of PHP 8, a project whose baseline offering was expanded to include fibers and even a Just In Time (JIT) compiler, Joe Watkins pulled the plug on support for the project. Furthermore, the API had grown to include more threading primitives—mutexes and a kill command, for example—that require more finesse to use effectively and increase proneness to all manner of haphazard parallel executions: pthreads had grown to ship more footguns. In light of the need to create an approach that not only enhances the share-nothing model, but also works in such a way as not to impede the PHP 8 JIT, ext-parallel and, with it, a CSP philosophy were introduced to the PHP userspace.

6.2.2 CSP and ext-parallel

With a share-nothing approach, essentially the intellection that informs the traditional threading model, memory sharing between threads executing in parallel happens by default. By virtue of existing in the same process, parallel units in a system like one created with pthreads can access data in a shared jurisdiction, but only with safeguards like symbol tables and mutexes that prevent data races. Ownership of resources accrues to all threads spawned from a process, therefore. The default threading model might not always scale effectively, however, as sharing memory, a precious resource, among potentially many threads upon instantiation can prove somewhat wasteful. Enter CSP. Formulated in 1977 by CAR Hoare and popularized by the Go programming language, CSP is a formal notation for representing an event-based synchronization of executable data units (or processes). It is based on the concept of linking inputs and outputs via an input target variable, which, in practice, initiates a memory-sharing operation between two otherwise isolated units: units that each own resources. By conferring data ownership on individual units, the means of synchronization is altered such that the safeguards present in the traditional share-nothing approach are eliminated in favor of conditional sharing of select data and, consequently, memory. Such sharing occurs only when an input command signals the availability of data that an output command can act on: when the event that serves as a precondition for communication is triggered. CSP is anchored on the following building blocks.

Processes that are synonymous with executable units or threads. Each process signifies a behavior that can be modeled into a capacious machine capable of parallelizing it. As far as the CSP notation goes, a process takes on the form of an uppercase lexeme sequence. A, B, and C are all stand-ins (aliases if you like) for disparate processes in this scheme that could as well have more elaborate names.

Events that are the individual actions that define a process. Every event defines an aspect of a process: something that can be executed. When listed in their entirety, that is, when the full range of atomic actions is presented, a process alphabet is formed. Notationally, an event is represented as a lowercase lexeme sequence and an alphabet as a set of such words. The alphabet for process A can be written as follows.

$$\alpha A = \{p, q, r\} \tag{6.1}$$

Traces that are definitive finite sequences of events. Every trace represents a predictable series of events consistent with the overall behavior of a process. A sequence for the process A, with events p, q, and r, can be represented as a comma-separated list of events encased in angle brackets, like so.

$$seq\ A = \langle p, q, r \rangle \tag{6.2}$$

p occurs before q and q before r in the trace shown.

Prefixes   that serve as the primitives on which to base the synchronization of data. In CSP, the words *prefix* and *guard* are used interchangeably. A prefix is a special event that, when used in an expression denoted in a manner similar to the path traversal in the previous chapter, serves as the precondition for the event or process that follows it to occur. It is the data that conditions synchronization between communicating processes, without which neither preceding nor proceeding processes can execute. A simple prefix p, an event in process A's alphabet that synchronizes processes A and B, can be written as follows.

$$A = p \rightarrow B \tag{6.3}$$

Channels   that act as the conduits for synchronization. They are bridges between processes. Schematically, a channel is a collection of input and output events, each with a corresponding source and destination. Each channel is responsible for enabling the action of a prefix in synchronizing communicating processes. If the prefix p is required to synchronize processes A and B and exists in the sequence $seq\,A$, the synchronization enabled by a channel designed to connect A and B can be written like so.

$$A|[\{p\}]|B \equiv p \rightarrow q \rightarrow r \rightarrow STOP \tag{6.4}$$

Notationally, this means that p serves as the guard whose presence initiates memory sharing between two resource-owning processes, A and B. In this arrangement, B is the target and A the source. Implied in the identity is the action of a channel in ensuring that, barring the execution of event p by both A and B, events q and r cannot occur.

With this information, it is possible to remodel the example from the previous segment as a full-fledged CSP subsystem. In a CSP regime, the two threads from earlier become two processes, *Post* and *Comments*, each with its own isolated runtime and total ownership of all the base resources of the PHP userspace—the artifacts (functions, objects, constants, etc.) that reside in the global namespace. Because the two processes have more or less the same algorithmic beats and are shaped by the same events, their alphabets and thus traces are also one and the same. Notationally, this shared alphabet can be written as follows.

$$\alpha Post = \alpha Comments = \{postid, httpfetch, jsondecode\} \tag{6.5}$$

The events *postid*, *httpfetch*, and *jsondecode* each describe the discrete actions that can be performed in each of the parallelizable units—Post and Comments. The first, *postid*, is short for the event in which a unique numerical identifier of a blog post is specified. *httpfetch* and *jsondecode*, respectively, represent an HTTP request to the Typicode service and the lossless conversion of a

JSON document to its PHP hashtable equivalent. Because the events in the alphabet occur in the order in which they are listed in each process, an appropriate shared trace can be written like so.

$$seq\ Post = seq\ Comments = \langle postid, httpfetch, jsondecode \rangle \qquad (6.6)$$

The behavior modeled in the previous example is such that the same post identifier is used for retrieving not only a blog entry, but also the comments associated with it. If the post identifier were to somehow be buffered between the two processes, then the event $postid$ would be considered a viable candidate for prefix status. In practice, however, both calls to the Typicode API for posts and comments must execute in full for any synchronization to occur. This behavior was demonstrated before, as the combined list of posts and comments created after synchronization was only created on full HTTP request completion and subsequent JSON-to-hashtable conversion. Because it is possible to send losslessly converted JSON over a channel and thence buffer it, the event $jsondecode$ can be assigned guard status and thus present the precondition for synchronization between $Post$ and $Comments$. Per the notational rules of CSP, this guard can be stated as shown below.

$$Post = jsondecode \rightarrow Comments \qquad (6.7)$$

Synchronization cannot occur sans channel in CSP. In accordance with all the rubric of the redesign discussed thus far, a fitting bridge between $Post$ and $Comments$ is one whose superstructure is made up entirely of the guard $postid$. This synchronization is the essence of any communication between the two processes and the gateway to realizing a system in which sharing memory only occurs while passing state—the mandate of CSP. Its canonical notational form appears as follows.

$$Post\|[\{jsondecode\}]\|Comments$$
$$\equiv postid \rightarrow httpfetch \rightarrow jsondecode \rightarrow STOP \qquad (6.8)$$

Now that all the requirements for synchronization have been notationally expressed, a PHP program can be written, atop ext-parallel, the second of two extensions written by Joe Watkins for the express purpose of sharing memory by communicating. ext-parallel embodies the philosophy of CAR Hoare and ships with the necessary primitives for parallelizing tasks per its notational guidelines—processes and channels. Processes are implemented in the extension as POSIX threads with resource ownership called runtimes that can be bootstrapped to include artifacts whose residency is in user-created PHP files. Channels, on the other hand, are objects with methods for buffering data and receiving buffered data. A simple program that synchronizes a post and its comments, which enacts an already established CSP notation, can be written like so.

Bridging Post and Comments with ext-parallel

```php
use parallel\{
  Channel,
  Runtime,
};

use function Chemem\Bingo\Functional\{
  Functors\Monads\IO\IO,
  fold,
  concat,
};

$channel = new Channel();

function getResource(
  int $postid,
  Channel $channel,
  bool $comments = false,
) {
  $runtime  = new Runtime();
  $url      = concat(
    '/',
    'https://jsonplaceholder.typicode.com/posts',
    (string) $postid,
    $comments ? 'comments' : '',
  );

  $runtime->run(
    function (string $url, Channel $channel): void {
      $channel->send(
        \json_decode(
          \file_get_contents($url),
          true,
        ),
      );
    },
    [$url, $channel],
  );

  return IO(
    $channel->recv(),
  );
}

$id     = 1;
$result = getResource($id, $channel)
  ->bind(
    fn (array $post) =>
      getResource($id, $channel, true)
        ->map(
          fn (array $comments): array =>
```

```
                [
                    ...$post,
                    'comments' => $comments,
                ],
            ),
        )
        ->exec();

    var_dump($result);

    $channel->close();
```

The function getResource serves as a pivotal abstraction in this reimagined subsystem. It is a handy abstraction from which a runtime can be created in which the events in the traces $seq Post$ and $seq Comments$ are executed and sent via a channel. Per the CSP model described in the preceding text, the data relayed via a channel is the hashtable version of the JSON result sent by Typicode's servers. Each time the server response is relayed by a runtime bootstrapped with `getResource`, memory is shared between communicating processes that have access to the channel in which the data is buffered. When partially applied and thus tied to a specific channel and the post identifier, 1, as in the assignment to the variable `$seq`, the function is primed for retrieving a single post and its comments in separate subsequent calls and the language engine running ext-parallel to share memory on the receipt of data buffered in a dedicated channel. To the variable `$result` is assigned a hashtable formed upon merging the data produced from the lazily evaluated, synchronized traces of $Post$ and $Comments$, a list that, like before, contains all post fields and a comments record.

It is important to remember that threads are no panacea. While they may provide increased throughput in several use cases, they can degrade algorithmic performance when spawned haphazardly. The decision to adopt any one of the aforediscussed threading philosophies, the latter being the preferable one because of its parsimony, should be informed in large part by the strenuousness of the problem, the solution for which stands to produce the biggest performance gains from divvying up repeatable parts.

6.3 Multiprocessing in PHP

As mentioned earlier, multiprocessing is a technique for which the mandate is decomposing tasks into dispatchable processes, each a unit of work scheduled by the kernel. Synchronizing processes requires a different philosophy that has more in common with traditional threading than it does with CSP and is an endeavor that very often performs slower than the recently covered analogous activity of synchronizing threads. Processes are prone to using more memory than threads and can only communicate via any one of a socket, semaphore, or message queue, artifacts that do not impede their ability to run separately. Such artifacts constitute a suite of tools considered appropriate for Inter-Process Communication (IPC), a mechanism for sharing data among independently running processes. Multiprocessing is only an option on Operating Systems that support a process model. Those that do not, like Windows, are considered unfit for multiprocessing.

> **Accessing Multiprocessing via WSL**

The Windows Subsystem for Linux, abbreviated WSL, is a Hyper-V virtualized Linux environment for Windows that allows those keen on using Linux distro utilities in Windows environments while retaining access to a shared filesystem. Newer versions of the technology allow for more than just terminal access to the process-rich environment that is Linux and now ship with support for some desktop applications. To access multiprocessing on Windows, consider downloading or building a WSL-siloed version of PHP complete with sysvshm and pcntl bindings.

Baked into most Linux systems, and transitively the PHP builds suited to running in their environments, is the fork model, considered the quintessential enabler of everything child process–related. To replicate the parallelization in the examples shown in both prior threading segments with processes, a working version of ext-pcntl, short for Process Control, and the extension ext-sysvshm, short for Shared Memory Segment, should be installed on a target system. Something like the following should work as an example of how to parallelize post and comment retrieval with processes.

Multiprocessing with ext-pcntl and ext-sysvshm

```php
use function Chemem\Bingo\Functional\{
  Functors\Monads\IO\IO,
  concat,
  partialRight,
};

\define('SEG_ID', 200);

function getResource(int $postid, bool $comments = false)
{
  return IO(
    \file_get_contents(
      concat(
        '/',
        'https://jsonplaceholder.typicode.com/posts',
        (string) $postid,
        $comments ? 'comments' : '',
      ),
    ),
```

```php
  );
}

$acc = [
  fn () => getResource(1),
  fn () => getResource(1, true),
];
$idx = 0;
$shm = \shm_attach(SEG_ID, 1024 * 512);

while ($action = $acc[$idx++] ?? null) {
  $pid = \pcntl_fork();

  if ($pid === -1) {
    \fwrite(
      STDERR,
      'Error forking process',
    );
    \exit(EXIT_FAILURE);
  }

  if ($pid === 0) {
    if ($idx === 1) {
      \shm_put_var($shm, $idx, $action()->exec());
      \exit(); // terminate child process
    }

    if ($idx == 2) {
      \shm_put_var($shm, $idx, $action()->exec());
      \exit(); // terminate child process
    }
  }
}

while (\pcntl_waitpid(0, $status) !== -1);

$decode = partialRight(
  \json_decode(...),
  true,
);

$posts    = \shm_get_var($shm, 1);
$comments = \shm_get_var($shm, 2);

var_dump(
  [
    ...$decode($posts),
    'comments' => $decode($comments),
  ],
);

\shm_detach($shm);
```

From a flow perspective, the example above describes a program such that the work in a reimagined version of `getResource` from before is spun off into two processes, one designated as the retriever of posts and the other a retriever of comments. Each of the aforementioned processes is terminated once its result is placed in a Shared Memory Segment before the eventual combination of process-retrieved posts and comments into a single table. Particularly intriguing here is the Shared Memory Segment, the API for which features functions with a distinctive prefix "shm."

Shared Memory Segments, or colloquially shms, are slices of RAM designed with the express intent of transiently buffering memory between communicating processes. They are readily implementable data fragments that require a numeric identifier and a size threshold (in bytes) on instantiation. Once created via a call to shm_attach, the fragment identified by the segment ID 200 is first used in the process labeled 1, before its termination, to buffer the result of a network call to the Typicode servers for the first post in a rich dataset. It is used again, and for the last time in the parent process, to buffer the comments relayed by process 2 for the same post. Upon termination of all child processes spawned, the variegated data in the segment 200 are retrieved via their respective numeric identifiers, 1 and 2, that correspond to those of the processes from which they were buffered.

Although processes are commonplace in the OSs that allow for them to be used, the potential fallout from using them incorrectly is massive. Processes live in the kernelspace and, as such, have access to more memory than threads. Haphazardly implemented multiprocessing schemes are prone to creating "fork bombs," bouts of system function impairment resulting from mass replication of processes. As with threads, great care needs to be taken when handling processes.

6.4   Message Brokerage with Evented I/O

Communicating is one of the throughlines of the discussions tabled thus far and a cornerstone idea in the world of concurrency. Sharing data among threads via synchronization primitives and between processes via IPC is, in effect, communicating. The thing about such communication is that it, for the most part, is constrained to a single environment—that of some kind of parent process, a single program that, in the case of multithreading, can be molded to spawn dispatchable, parallelly executable userspace-residing units and, in a multiprocessing regime, child processes that are just as parallelizable albeit with different communication primitives. The communication achievable with message brokerage is one that seeks to connect processes in an architecture, at the core of which is a dedicated message dispatcher responsible for sending messages between senders and recipients. This dispatcher, a message broker, is an autonomous system, unlike threads and child processes that are mostly consigned to a single parent process.

A message broker is typically designed to be resilient and fluent in relaying messages encoded in a parsable, generalized message format—a protocol. Resilience here is the ability to maintain the capacity to function while withstanding the rigors of an operating environment. Many a message broker is hardened against channel failures that can manifest as jitter and intermittency and protocol-related snafus that may originate from corrupt messages. Internally, brokers implement a queue such that messages pulsed through them are sent out in the order that they were received, to their intended designated recipients. The queueing in such systems is typically asynchronous, meaning that a sender and designated recipient do not have to be running at the same exact time and can more or less take on the roles of publisher, a process that sends data to the queue, and dedicated subscriber, a process that listens for messages sent to the queue. Any process written in any language, C, PHP, JavaScript, Lisp, and what have you, can, provided it is able to access a broker and encode message relay instructions in a relevant messaging protocol, be sculpted into either a producer or consumer. On that note, it is possible to segue into discussing an efficient means of writing producers and consumers, with evented I/O.

6.4.1 Evented I/O

Briefly introduced in Chapter 4 and referenced by another equally descriptive name, evented I/O is a paradigm entirely concerned with leveraging the OS kernel, via system calls, to interleave the results of Input/Output expressions and minimize CPU idleness between consecutive tasks. The system calls made by evented systems do not condition the creation of separate work units (threads, processes, and the like), and so, such systems are generally suited to running in the single thread from which the requisite system calls are made. The asynchrony in evented I/O is such that evented expressions do not always immediately return a result when called, as the CPU is kept busy by them and can defer its evaluations of every request it receives in such a way as to service each request gradually while receiving others. This is best exemplified by the component at the heart of every evented system, known as an event loop. This artifact dispatches user I/O actions to the CPU by way of the kernel and, on each CPU execution readiness state change, the results of each such action via appropriate user-defined functions. Interactions with evented I/O typically involve passing data around as a stream, a structure built to effect unbuffered flows of its constituent chunks from point to point, or as a primitive in a promise already discussed in Chapter 4. In PHP, async tools like those in ReactPHP (also discussed in Chapter 4) and Amp can help infuse regular programs with asynchronous, evented dispatch.

Demonstrating Pub/Sub with Evented I/O

For the demonstration in this section, the retrieval of posts and comments from earlier is adjusted to fit a message brokerage involving a publisher and subscriber, such that the publisher enqueues a blog post identifier in a message broker that the subscriber, actively listening for updates, then generates a combined list for. The popular key–value store Redis will feature as the message broker in this demonstration. Defined in its Redis Serialization Protocol (RESP), a presentation layer protocol that sits atop TCP in the network stack, are conventions for message passing between publisher and subscriber that, in the demonstration to follow, will be depicted as two PHP scripts each running an instance of an evented (non-blocking) RESP client.

With the goals for the closed message brokerage set, the development of a suitable publisher–subscriber system can begin. First up in the system to create is the producer. In this demonstration, it is a simple program whose expressions reside in the file named "producer.php." This producer is implemented as a simple script to which a blog post identifier to be enqueued can be passed as a command-line argument. It is written in such a way as to establish a connection with the message broker and relay the post identifier it receives via the PUBLISH RESP command, a facility for publishing a message on a dedicated channel. The channel here is simply a label for a specific queue on which to publish messages, which, for purposes of this demonstration, is named "blog." It can therefore be asserted that the producer's design is an encoding of the intent to publish post IDs and thence enqueue them in a "blog" queue. The producer looks like this.

Producer in a Simple Pub/Sub System

```php
// producer.php
use Clue\React\Redis\Factory;

$redis  = (new Factory())
  ->createLazyClient('localhost:6379');
$postid = $argv[1] ?? '1';

$redis
  ->publish('blog', $postid)
  ->then(
    function () use ($postid): void {
      echo \sprintf("Sent ID %s to consumer\n", $postid);
    },
    function (Throwable $err): void {
      echo \sprintf(
        "Unable to publish because %s\n",
        $err->getMessage(),
      );

      \exit(1);
    },
  );
```

Next is the consumer, the subscriber in this pub/sub message brokerage system. Defined in a file named "consumer.php" are expressions that enable active monitoring of the "blog" channel in a subscription such that with every receipt of a post identifier enqueued and subsequently dequeued by the broker, a download of a corresponding post and its comments is effected. The consumer is wired to download a post and its comments every time it receives an identifier in a parallel fashion, after establishing a connection to the broker and initiating the aforedescribed real-time subscription via the RESP command SUBSCRIBE. This parallel fetching is enabled via the evented I/O function named `all` that conditions the simultaneous processing of all deferred actions in promises passed to it. The consumer script takes on the following form.

Consumer in a Simple Pub/Sub System

```php
// consumer.php
use Clue\React\Redis\Factory;
use React\Http\Browser;

use function React\Promise\all;

$redis = (new Factory())
  ->createLazyClient('localhost:6379');

$channel = 'blog';
$redis
  ->subscribe($channel)
  ->then(
    function () use ($channel): void {
      echo \sprintf("Subscribed to channel %s\n", $channel);
    },
    function (Throwable $err) use ($channel, $redis): void {
      $redis->close();

      echo \sprintf(
        "Could not subscribe to channel %s because %s\n",
        $channel,
        $err->getMessage(),
      );
    },
  );

$redis->on(
  'message',
  function (string $channel, string $message): void {
    echo \sprintf("Received id %s\n", $message);

    $browser  = new Browser();
    $browser  = $browser->withBase(
      \sprintf('https://jsonplaceholder.typicode.com', $message),
    );
    $browser = $browser->withHeader(
      'content-type',
```

```php
      'application/json; charset=utf-8',
  );
  $decode    = fn (object $response): array =>
    \json_decode(
      (string) $response->getBody(),
      true,
    );

  all(
    [
      'post'        => $browser
        ->get(
          \sprintf('/posts/%s', $message),
        )
        ->then($decode),
      'comments'  => $browser
        ->get(
          \sprintf('/posts/%s/comments', $message),
        )
        ->then($decode),
    ],
  )
    ->then(
      function (array $responses): void {
        [
          'post'       => $post,
          'comments'  => $comments,
        ] = $responses;

        \var_dump(
          [
            ...$post,
            'comments' => $comments,
          ],
        );
      },
      function (Throwable $err): void {
        echo \sprintf(
          "%s: Could not download contents\n",
          $err->getMessage(),
        );
      },
    );
  },
);
```

Now that two out of three components required to operationalize the closed system have been defined, it is possible to start the broker, the enabler of message relay between publisher and subscriber. In a console window, type the command `redis-server` to instantiate a Redis process that, by default, will listen on port 6379 of the loopback address 127.0.0.1. Something like Figure 6.1 should appear in the window as a signifier of a successful launch attempt.

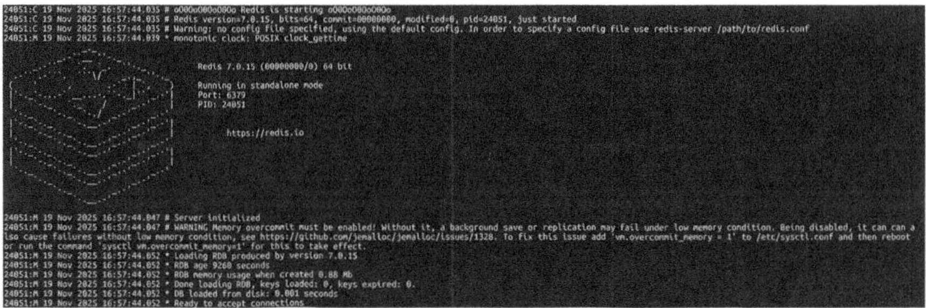

Fig. 6.1 Successful launch of Redis server

Fig. 6.2 Successful subscription to "blog" channel

Fig. 6.3 Send operation performed upon running producer program

Next, in a separate window, instantiate the consumer via the console directive `php consumer.php`. It is a long-running process like the broker that should, on successful instantiation, print the message "Subscribed to channel blog," like Figure 6.2.

To send an identifier via producer, in yet another console window, the directive `php producer.php {id}` should suffice. The post identifier 1, used in the preceding chapter segments, can be sent via console like Figure 6.3.

Turning your attention to the window in which the consumer is running will reveal the same combined list from previous examples, after a message that reads "Received id 1" is printed by the consumer to the console's Standard Output. The updated consumer display appears as shown in Figure 6.4.

It is worth noting that the brokerage shown in this segment is scalable because it simulates a design pattern in which expensive I/O operations, such as network requests, are offloaded to a process dedicated to servicing them. Deferring work like this makes it possible to reserve resource bandwidth in a foreground-running publisher that could be busied with servicing several requests.

There you have it—techniques mightily useful in increasing the throughput of PHP applications that also happen to be congruous with the principles of Functional Programming. Consider using any one or a combination of multithreading, multiprocessing, or message brokerage to write high-performance PHP applications in an idiomatic way, without utilizing more tools than what you can avail yourself of in the language userspace. Featured in the next chapter are techniques that are doubly useful in the context of Functional Programming: first, as concepts that are interoperable with everything discussed thus far and, second, as ideas that further emphasize the pragmatism of composition as a technique that can readily be plugged into a host of everyday scenarios.

```
Received id 1
array(5) {
  ["userId"]=>
  int(1)
  ["id"]=>
  int(1)
  ["title"]=>
  string(74) "sunt aut facere repellat provident occaecati excepturi optio reprehenderit"
  ["body"]=>
  string(158) "quia et suscipit
suscipit recusandae consequuntur expedita et cum
reprehenderit molestiae ut ut quas totam
nostrum rerum est autem sunt rem eveniet architecto"
  ["comments"]=>
  array(5) {
    [0]=>
    array(5) {
      ["postId"]=>
      int(1)
      ["id"]=>
      int(1)
      ["name"]=>
      string(28) "id labore ex et quam laborum"
      ["email"]=>
      string(18) "Eliseo@gardner.biz"
      ["body"]=>
      string(148) "laudantium enim quasi est quidem magnam voluptate ipsam eos
tempora quo necessitatibus
dolor quam autem quasi
reiciendis et nam sapiente accusantium"
    }
    [1]=>
    array(5) {
      ["postId"]=>
      int(1)
      ["id"]=>
      int(2)
      ["name"]=>
      string(41) "quo vero reiciendis velit similique earum"
      ["email"]=>
      string(22) "Jayne_Kuhic@sydney.com"
      ["body"]=>
      string(168) "est natus enim nihil est dolore omnis voluptatem numquam
et omnis occaecati quod ullam at
voluptatem error expedita pariatur
nihil sint nostrum voluptatem reiciendis et"
    }
    [2]=>
    array(5) {
```

Fig. 6.4 Parallel fetch operation performed by consumer upon receipt of post ID

Chapter 7
Additional Functional Programming Techniques

7.1 Lenses

When interacting with a composite data structure such as a hashtable, there is a high likelihood of writing functions to retrieve specific data that resides inside it and modify parts of the entire structure. These functions, termed getters and setters, respectively, are commonplace state-shaping utilities in PHP code and can weigh down the development process with additional modificative effort when a state change occurs. Consider the example below.

Depiction of Tandem Use of a Setter and Getter

```
$usernames = [
  'ace411',
  'agiroLoki',
  'loki',
];

$getFirst = fn (array $list): mixed => $list[0] ?? null;
$setFirst = function (string $name, array $list): array {
  $list[0] = $name;

  return $list;
};
$updated  = $setFirst('@ace411', $usernames);

var_dump(
  $getFirst($updated),
);
```

© The Author(s), under exclusive license to APress Media, LLC,
part of Springer Nature 2026
M. B. Lochemem, *Functional Programming in PHP*,
https://doi.org/10.1007/979-8-8688-2468-5_7

Defined above are a list of usernames, a getter named $getFirst with which to retrieve the first item in the aforementioned list, and a setter named $setFirst with which to overwrite and thence update the username slotted into the first numeric index of the same list. When the second of the duo of aforedescribed functions is called to update the first username entry with a version of itself prefixed with the symbol "@", a value that is subsequently accessed via the getter $getFirst, then a get–set sequence will have been executed successfully under the assumption that the rules governing the use of the list of usernames dictate that the first value is that slotted into the list at index 0. If the rules were ever to change to dictate, say, a more definitive key-based approach for the list of usernames wherein all values are inserted into slots that correspond to string identifiers, particularly services for which the usernames are valid, then modifications across the board to all getters and setters would be warranted. A program that captures the aforedescribed rule changes could look like so.

Rewrite of Getter–Setter Pair from Earlier

```
$usernames = [
  'github'    => 'ace411',
  'x'         => 'agiroLoki',
  'web'       => 'loki',
];


$getFirst = fn (array $list): mixed => $list['github'] ?? null;
$setfirst = function (string $username, array $list): array {
  $list['github'] = $username;

  return $list;
};
```

The key "github" is treated as the first element in this reimagined version of the username state-shaping program. In this new regime, the getter and setter from before, $getFirst and $setFirst, originally tethered to the idea of using numeric indexes, are rewritten entirely in acclimation to the new rules. While the change depicted above is not a cumbersome adjustment, as only one pair of getters and setters is modified, the effort required in repurposing multiple pairs of getters and setters, such as those that would be required for the second and third elements of the list, would make for a tedious change. Reducing this tedium would require writing generic getters and setters that parameterize keys to guarantee precision in targeting a specific part of a composite state. Something like the following could suffice in this regard.

Depiction of Generic Getter–Setter Pair

```
$get = fn (array $list, string|int $key): mixed =>
  $list[$key] ?? null;
$set = function (
  string $key,
  string $username,
  array $list,
): array {
  $list[$key] = $username;

  return $list;
};
```

The functions shown above are generic in the sense that they obviate the need for duplicative effort in acclimating multiple getter–setter pairs to new rules. The genericness of the lambdas $get and $set applies only to hashtables and not other types of composite structures of which there are many in the PHP userspace— queues, heaps, generators, and so on. Even arbitrarily abstract structures like those whose logics are defined in classes, depending on the extent to which their properties can be manipulated, are candidates for the application of the genericness in the pair shown above. To fill this need for genericness in composite states are lenses, structures with which to sharply target portions of rich structures with composable getter–setter pairs like $get and $set above.

A lens is a functorial structure made up of a getter–setter function pair designed with the sole intent of focusing on a particular, typically smaller part of an abstract composite state. Edward Kmett, a Haskell programmer whose pioneering work popularized the idea of composing pairs of generic getters and setters, modeled the programmatic lens in computer science after the concept of the concave lens in physics, which forms a small image at its principal focus when light from an object placed at infinity is reflected onto its surface. With a lens, it is possible not only to retrieve an item at a point of focus as well as set and thus wholly update a value or retrieve data from a composite structure, but also to apply more detailed, arbitrary modifications to data that constitutes a richer state. Using a lens means that adjusting to state changes like the one specified in the rule change described earlier means updating the target of the lens without necessarily changing the entire scaffolding. The program from earlier that showcased the use of a getter–setter pair on a list containing numerically indexed usernames can be rewritten in such a way as to replicate the result achieved by using a setter and getter in tandem, but only after funneling them into a lens and invoking the set and view functions defined in its API. It can be reimagined, with a lens, like so.

Depiction of a Simple Lens

```php
use function Chemem\Bingo\Functional\Functors\Lens\{
  lens,
  set,
  view,
};

$usernames = [
  'ace411',
  'agiroLoki',
  'loki',
];

$getFirst = fn (array $list): mixed => $list[0] ?? null;
$setFirst = function (string $name, array $list): array {
  $list[0] = $name;

  return $list;
};
$lens       = lens($getFirst, $setFirst);
$updated    = set(
  $lens,
  '@ace411',
  $usernames,
);

var_dump(
  view($lens, $updated),
);
```

The function lens, when invoked, appropriately creates a lens from the getter
and setter passed to it. In practice, a lens is little more than a higher-order function:
the last lambda in a sequence of returned closures that creates a functor from the
getter and maps over it with the setter. Calling the function set performs the same
overwrite demonstrated before, while calling view simply returns the focus of the
lens, the new value at index 0—"@ace411". In addition to the lens function that
allows for the use of an arbitrary getter–setter pair to shape the focus of a lens, the
bingo-functional ships with generic accessors that cover several use cases, typically
those that are relevant to list-like structures. Applying such accessors can produce
shorter forms and thus eliminate the need for the pair $getFirst and $setFirst.
The function lensKey is one such generic lens that simply allows those intent on
using it to focus on a specific index, numeric or otherwise, in a manipulable store.
Replacing the call to lens with lensKey, as in the example below, can produce a
more compact program.

Depiction of a Terser Lens

```
use function Chemem\Bingo\Functional\Functors\Lens\{
  lensKey,
  set,
  view,
};

$lens      = lensKey(0);
$updated   = set(
  $lens,
  '@ace411',
  $usernames,
);

var_dump(
  view($lens, $updated),
);
```

Tidied inside of `lensKey` is a generic getter–setter pair that works not only on hashtables, but also on objects. It is a handy abstraction that is amenable to changes to the rules surrounding the nature of accessible keys, as any real modification to a key regime would simply require a trivial parameter change for the lens to retain viability. This speaks to the general parsimony of lenses as small changes in the requirements of a program that features them condition commensurately small changes in the building blocks of constituent lenses affected by the changes.

It is worth mentioning that the mechanics of retrieval and modification in a lens, with getters and setters, respectively, are bound by laws that ensure consistent behavior. These laws are as follows:

1. Attempting to access the focal point of a lens via a view operation upon successfully updating the said focus in a set operation will produce the result of the update. This law is canonically written as follows.

$$view\, l\ (set\, l\ x) = x \tag{7.1}$$

x in this case is the value placed in focus—the subject of the update.

2. Overwriting the value in the focus of a lens after a successful update of the same focal point produces the same result as updating the focus once, with the value assigned on overwrite. Simply put, setting twice is the same as setting once with the value passed to the most recent set operation. This can be expressed as follows.

$$set\, s\ y\ .\ set\, s\ x = set\, s\ y \tag{7.2}$$

x is the value placed in focus initially, and y is the value placed in focus on overwrite.

3. Setting the focus of a lens to the value in focus leaves the state it is applied to unchanged. Canonically, this is expressed like so.

$$set\, l\ (view\, l\ z)\ z = z \qquad (7.3)$$

z here denotes the state shaped by the lens l.

As mentioned earlier, a lot more than just setting and getting with the respective functions set and view can be done with a lens. The function over, a staple of virtually all lens APIs, makes it possible to fully harness the map operation in the functor at the heart of a lens. Calling it is a means of effecting targeted discretionary changes to the focal point of a lens beyond simple overwrites. If there were ever to arise a need to append to the third username entry in the same list as before, the "@" symbol and a domain name, and thence convert it to a full-on email address, the over function would supersede the overwrite operation, set, because of its ability to offer more control to produce a desired result. Please turn your attention to the depiction below.

Demonstration of the Use of Over to Apply Append Operation to Lens Focus

```
use function Chemem\Bingo\Functional\Functors\Lens\{
  lensKey,
  over,
  view,
};

// refer to the list of usernames specified in a previous example

$lens    = lensKey(2);
$updated = over(
  $lens,
  fn (string $username): string => \sprintf('%s@chemem.site', $username),
  $usernames,
);

var_dump(
  view($lens, $updated),
);
```

The function over, unlike set, takes a unary modificative function as a second parameter, the sole argument for which is the value currently in focus—the entry stored in the $usernames hashtable in the slot 2 in this case. In applying the said function to the value "loki" to create the email address "loki@chemem.site," the over function acts as a proxy for the map method described in Chapter 5 of this book. It, therefore, serves as the basis for all attempts at modifying the focus of a lens, including the operation `set`. In fact, all calls to `set` are, internally, calls to `over` with a constant function to which an arbitrary value intended for placement at the principal focus of a lens is passed. Lenses are easy to use on various kinds of composite states and with an intuitive API can be purposed to create compact, reusable state-shaping abstractions.

7.2 Recursion

Recursion is a pattern that features functions calling themselves. It is, in terms of effect, very similar to iteration via control structure (`if/else`, `do/while`, and the like), but has some unique fundamental preconditions for success. For any attempt at recursion to succeed, a base case and well-articulated sub-cases to be executed in each iteration should be spelled out. A base case is, in the context of recursion, a special expression that serves as the stipulation upon which termination of repeat calls to the same function should cease: it is the termination clause for recursion. Sub-cases, on the other hand, are **effective** decompositions of a problem that can be solved via iteration. A workable sub-case is effectively a well-defined, repeatable portion of a workload in an iterative sequence that is not prone to creating wasteful, repetitive cycles.

A function that produces a Fibonacci number, already showcased in this text, is a commonplace example of recursion. Its design is such that, on invocation, it automatically evaluates to the value supplied to it if the said value is less than 2 and repeatedly computes, through a fitting number of calls to itself, for every value greater than 2, the sum of the differences between a number, greater in magnitude than the one before it, and the values 1 and 2, a contextual result with **no repeat cases**. The former is the function's base case, whereas the latter is a description of the non-cyclical sub-steps required in producing the desired result—a valid Fibonacci number. This information is exemplified by the call to a recursive function `fib`, with the value 9, which produces the number 34.

Recursion with Fibonacci Function

```
$fib = function (int $val) use (&$fib): int {
  return $val < 2 ?
    $val :
    $fib($val - 1) + $fib($val - 2);
};

var_dump($fib(9));
```

It is possible to write the map operation discussed in Chapter 3 as a recursive function. As a recursive function, map's base case is a situation where the end of the list has been reached. Because this condition is easiest to check for when working with lists whose keys are numeric, the simplest form of a recursive variant of map, it can be asserted, works best when used on such hashtables. The result of the recursive variant, also an array, is updated with each disparate non-cyclical application of the function passed to it and retained through successive self-calls to the current item in the hashtable, to which the function's internal counter points. Please turn your attention to the implementation named `mapr`, short for `map-recursive`, that exemplifies this recursive behavior.

> Avoid Needless Calls to Count

While it might seem tempting to call the function `count` in situations where it is convenient to compute the size of a list so as to factor it into some kind of follow-up evaluation, like in the snippet to follow, the endeavor, and thus the program in which it is expressed, might incur the algorithmic penalty of an additional iteration cycle. It is important to be mindful of this pitfall when designing iterative sequences in recursive contexts or otherwise, as extra cycles in expressions involving large lists can encumber performance.

Recursive Map Function

```
function mapr(
  callable $func,
  array $list,
  array $acc  = [],
  int $idx    = 0,
): array {
  if (!isset($list[$idx])) {
    return $acc;
  }

  $acc = [
    ...$acc,
    $func($list[$idx]),
  ];
  $idx += 1;

  return mapr(
    $func,
    $list,
    $acc,
    $idx,
  );
}
```

```
var_dump(
  mapr(
    fn (int $x): int => \pow($x, 2),
    \range(1, 5),
  ),
);
```

The recursion in `mapr` shown above, but really all recursion, incurs a cost. It heightens the risk of memory failures from stack frame sprawl. A stack frame, a composite structure that includes a function name and its arguments, is an entry in a function call stack that is populated in each running instance of PHP. Every function in the jurisdiction of the PHP interpreter, in its userspace and C engine, is assigned such a frame. When executing a recursive call, the C interpreter registers a new stack frame for each self-call in a recursive chain, in what is an $O(n)$ stack push operation. Several recursive calls, therefore, per this premise, condition the issuance of several frames that can bloat an otherwise clean stack and create memory problems that can deter the execution of a program. Though it is exceedingly difficult to remove the penalties of recursion without raising memory limits, there exist strategies to somewhat mitigate the penalties it inflicts.

Tail Call Optimization

The first mitigatory strategy, Tail Call Optimization (TCO), is applied upon compiling PHP. This compiler-centric TCO most profoundly improves the performance of C instructions in the PHP language interpreter and has little enhancive effect on tail-recursive userspace functions like `mapr`. The technique is especially effective because it produces leaner assembly code. Whenever a function is called, the Program Counter (PC), a special register in the CPU, points to the next executable address, typically that of the caller to which control is returned upon completion of execution. The assembly directives `CALL`, which invokes a function; `RET`, which returns the address of the stack pointed to by `CALL`; and `JMP`, the directive that updates the PC value to that of the next executable instruction like a `goto` statement would direct the flow of a program to a specified destination section, are executed in that order when a function is called. TCO eliminates `CALL` and `RET` from the slate of assembly instructions of a function with a tail call, resulting in a single `JMP` and, thus, a single operation that defers control to the next instruction, which is the next function to execute. It sets the PC's value to the stack address of the function designated as returnable, thereby creating a smaller tail call footprint. TCO is enabled by default in most PHP builds, which are compiled with the flag `\-On` where n denotes a level of optimization supported by a compiler.

Trampolines

The second ameliorative approach is centered around using trampolines to manage recursing state. Trampolines enable the reuse of stack frames by funneling function calls into a single, re-entrant callable unit. Re-entrant here is synonymous with possessing the capacity to be executed more than once while retaining the same call stack entry registered on initial invocation. Each time a re-entrant function is called, its result is that of a different function call in a recursive sequence. Trampolines only work on tail-recursive functions, such as `mapr`, and exist in PHP's Virtual Machine (VM) as well as its userspace.

In the PHP VM, the routine `execute_ex` serves as the re-entrant function into which PHP opcodes are shuttled. PHP opcodes are akin to the directives mentioned in the previous paragraph, but are language-specific simulations of CPU behavior: they are quasi-assembly instructions whose definitions are especially suited to executable constructs in the language. `execute_ex` is written in such a way as to ensure that PHP-specific CALL and RET directives are retained in a closed loop, an attunement that significantly reduces the likelihood of proliferating stack frames throughout the engine. Like TCO, the trampolines in the Zend engine are enabled by default in most builds. They are complemented by userspace solutions like the trampoline function below that is a constituent of the bingo-functional library.

Trampoline in PHP Userspace

```php
function trampoline(callable $func): callable
{
  $finalArgs = [];
  $recursing = false;

  return function (...$args) use (
    $func,
    &$finalArgs,
    &$recursing,
  ) {
    $finalArgs[] = $args;

    if (!$recursing) {
      $recursing = true;

      while (!empty($finalArgs)) {
        $result = $func(
          ...\array_shift($finalArgs),
        );
      }

      $recursing = false;
    }

    return $result;
  };
}
```

In the higher-order function depicted, its return value, a simple closure, provides the re-entrancy needed to effect trampoline behavior. It curbs the sprawl of stack frames in the PHP VM by acting like a thunk and effectively forwarding all recursive calls into its own signature. A chain of successive, thunk-contained recursive calls to an anonymous function is effectively started by passing an argument destined for the recursive function passed, in a preceding call, to the function whose signature it resides in by value, to the closure. Once inside the jurisdiction of the thunk, any arguments from the initial call to the recursive function are pushed into a list called `$finalArgs` and, subsequently, a loop from which they are popped when the function is recursing. When applied to a tail-recursive map operation aimed at computing the squares of 1,000 numbers in the range of 1,000–2,000, the trampoline function shown can achieve throughput that is not too far off from what more resource-efficient iteration is capable of offering. Something like the content of the following snippet demonstrates how to achieve the aforementioned optimization.

Using a Trampoline to Optimize a Tail-Recursive Map Operation

```
use function Chemem\Bingo\Functional\trampoline;

$mapr = trampoline(
  mapr(...),
);

var_dump(
  $mapr(
    fn (int $val): int => \pow($val, 2),
    \range(1000, 2000),
  ),
);
```

In truth, userspace trampolines offer little enhancive value as most of the work is done internally by `execute_ex`. They do, however, provide some insight into the re-entrancy achieved in modern versions of the PHP VM in addition to the marginal performance gains PHP users can avail themselves of when attempting to perform tail recursion at scale. Generally, recursion works best when used as a complement to iteration via control structure—`while`, `foreach`, `for`, and the like—and rarely as a first option despite the enhancements to more recent versions of the PHP engine that renders the technique viable for a wide range of tasks.

7.3 Pattern Matching

Not to be confused with regular expression matching, pattern matching is a means of evaluating whether data of a certain composition is likely to take on a form encoded as a template, a boilerplate representative of such fragmented composition. It is a means of checking if a unit of data has a characteristically descriptive form.

Any unit of data that takes on a predictable form is a good applicative surface for pattern matching. Everything from simple data like strings and numbers to abstractly defined objects can be reasoned about by applying pattern matching. The technique is a fixture in the designs of languages like Haskell and Elm, but is only actualizable as something that approximates its maximal form with additional plumbing in PHP. Outside of the match syntax introduced in PHP 8, there are scarce resources for pattern matching in PHP. The suite of pattern matching tools in the "bingo-functional" and "pattern-matching" libraries, the latter of which is the brainchild of Gilles Crettenand, mostly suffice as viable contextual tools that approximate the fullness of the technique, for they both offer facsimiles of Haskell pattern matching syntax and also enable pattern-based value extraction.

Often, when a discussion on pattern matching is broached, comparisons with the switch statement are made, and for good reason. The switch statement, a pervasive control structure in languages like PHP, is often used to differentiate discernible selections. It, like pattern matching, is used for flow control, but does not allow for evaluations of elaborate, characteristically distinct data. Using the switch statement to select from one of several intricate units of data in a composite structure like a list, in one go, is not a good proposition. The rule of thumb with a switch statement is that if the entropy of evaluable options falls outside of a set of basic primitives like a string or integer, then a more accommodating control flow structure should be opted for. Furthermore, the result of a switch statement is neither directly assignable to a single variable nor usable as a return value outright, as its case syntax is often adapted to scenarios defined by filling out predefined placeholders (variables) with scoped data. Pattern matching circumvents these limitations while also allowing for conditional extraction of state fragments from data subject to pattern-based evaluation. The technique is often described by those familiar with it as a "better switch statement."

Patterns are observable groupings of data that are either primitive, that is, limited to a single value like a string or integer, or tree-like and complex and thus composable from multiple primitives. A URL, for instance, is a tree pattern. Not only does it contain a scheme, but it also features a hostname, a port, a path, and occasionally a combination of a username and password, or even a fragment. When designing cases to be evaluated via pattern matching, one must be mindful of the duality of refutability, a concept that informs the treatment of successful and errant matches. An irrefutable match signifies a pattern that applies to all data in a selection. Expressions that reside in the global state of a program are considered irrefutable, for example, as the scoping rules they are bound by ensure their accessibility throughout the same program. Refutable matches, however, are exclusive to particular units of data in a selection and can fail to match when evaluated against others in the same selection. A pattern that can be notationally expressed as ["foo", "bar"] exclusively matches the string "foobar" but not "foo-bar" and can be categorized as refutable.

For a demonstration of pattern matching in PHP, a simple router that simulates one found in a run-of-the-mill blog can suffice. Centered on the retrieval of instances of a post resource, the distinct routes, essentially disparate path components in

Table 7.1 Summary of routes

Path	Purpose
/posts	Retrieves all posts
/post/{id}	Retrieves a post that matches a specified identifier

a URL that are passed along with controller functions as arguments to higher-order functions whose sole purpose is to operationalize controllers in more practical networking environments, can be summarized in Table 7.1.

The router to which the tabular information above is relevant features two posts coded into a simple in-memory registry, as well as a function named router into which the pattern matching is abstracted. All targeted retrievals are performed via a lens, and the data relay format is an idiomatic hashtable since there is no network interface, the presence of which would warrant lossless conversion of posts to a generalized media format. The simple router can be written as follows.

> Pattern Matching Syntax in PHP

Because PHP is not as syntactically well suited to pattern matching as, say, Haskell or OCaml or Elm, the workaround and thus standard enforced in most APIs in PHP centers around representing evaluable cases, pattern templates in hashtables. Hashtables have a particular key–value orientation useful for expressing pattern–action pairs, the latter of which is an n-ary function to evaluate on a successful match, that typify pattern matching in the languages known for offering it out of the box. Their $O(1)$ algorithmic efficiency also makes the case-driven evaluatory logic in the tools they reside in a lot less strenuous on the language engine.

For the most part, all the pattern templates used in pattern matching syntaxes are strings that are processed internally with PHP's potent compiled regex utilities. They constitute a Domain-Specific Language (DSL) in PHP, modeled after Haskell's matching system, in which there exist two core rule groups in addition to six primitives. The primitives are enumerated as follows:

1. **Strings** that are templates for exact matches to those written in PHP. As far as pattern matching is concerned, such data are represented as units enclosed in double quotes. The template " 'foo' ", per the DSL, is a template for a refutable match to the string "foo". All data encodable as strings in PHP, including canonical class and function names, can be matched against string templates.
2. **Integers** that are templates for data of the same type in PHP. The template '9' signifies a refutable match to the integer 9.
3. **Floating-point numbers** that, like integers, are also templates of the same type in PHP. The template '2.33' is an exact match for the floating-point number 2.33.
4. **Booleans** that are templates for true and false as used in the language userspace. The templates 'true' and 'false' exclusively depict the values true and false in PHP.

5. **A wildcard** that is a template for a an irrefutable, match-all pattern. Denoted as '_', the wildcard is used to signify a match to all possible patterns.
6. **A generic identifier** that is effectively a placeholder for data whose real value need not be represented in a pattern. Such primitives take on the form of lexeme sequences that are neither strings nor booleans, like the template 'a', which is a stand-in for an unspecified but present unit of data. The undisclosed values represented by identifiers are passed to the n-ary functions that correspond to the patterns in which they are featured.

Rule groups, like composite structures in PHP, build atop the aforelisted primitives and are especially useful when matching against data placed in lists. They are as follows:

1. **Cons**, a tree-like unit that works to destructure an array with generic identifiers and is written in such a way as to mark the separations between contiguous array parts with a prepend operator (:). The cons template "(x:xs)", for example, simply denotes a list with two elements and will, on a successful match with a list containing exactly two elements, forward those entries to the case-evaluative n-ary function to which it corresponds.
2. **Array**, which allows for more granular refutable matches against data in a list. It is the ruleset with the largest match entropy and allows for the nesting of all manner of combinations that reflect the nature of data in an input set. Array templates are always enclosed in square brackets like the sequence '["foo", (x), b]' that will match an array whose contents are the string "foo", a singleton array, and a third, undisclosed, arbitrary value like null, in that order.

Simple Router Implemented via Pattern Matching

```
use function Chemem\Bingo\Functional\{
  Functors\Lens\lensKey,
  Functors\Lens\view,
  PatternMatching\patternMatch as pmatch,
};

\define(
  'POSTS',
  [
    [
      'title' => 'Pattern Matching rocks!',
      'text'  => 'One can write better switch statements with it.',
    ],
    [
      'title' => 'Pattern Matching is simple!',
      'text'  => 'The PHP version uses intuitive Haskell syntax.',
    ],
  ],
);
```

```
function router(string $path): array
{
  return pmatch(
    [
      '["post", id]'  => fn (int $id): array =>
        view(
          lensKey($id - 1),
          POSTS,
        ) ??
        [
          'error' => \sprintf('The post %d does not exist', $id),
        ],
      '["posts"]'      => fn (): array => POSTS,
      '_'              => fn (): array =>
        [
          'error' => 'The resource does not exist',
        ],
    ],
    \explode(
      '/',
      \ltrim($path, '/'),
    ),
  );
}
```

Defined in the example above are two refutable patterns and one irrefutable one. Each refutable pattern in the pattern table shown corresponds to a route in the routes table relevant to the simple blog. The irrefutable pattern, on the other hand, is simply a cautionary case similar to the default clause in a switch or match control block, designated as the catch-all for all irrelevant matches and the pattern to evaluate in the event of a total failure.

Of the two refutable patterns, each an array template, the first, whose definition is '["post", id]', provides a means of matching against all valid requests that contain the string primitive 'post' and an identifier. For each successful match with this route pattern, the post identifier passed to the router is relayed to a unary function wherein a lens, the focus of which is the registry of posts, is formed and the value in its focal point, the post at a specified index in the registry, is extracted. In the event that an invalid index is computed by the function, an array containing an error message that reads 'The post id does not exist' is returned. Each match with the second of the duo of refutable patterns, a singleton with the sole value "posts", on the other hand, returns all entries in the registry.

To test whether the pattern matching enforces the constraints specified in the routes table, the following calls, each with a distinct relevant input, a route subject to the comparisons in the router, can suffice as an addendum to the program shown above.

Table 7.2 Summary of results produced by each evaluable route

Path	Purpose
/post/2	The post whose title reads "Pattern Matching is simple!"
/posts	The entire posts registry
/post/5	An array containing an error message that reads "The post 5 does not exist"
/comments/2	An array containing an error message that reads "The resource does not exist"

Evaluable Routing Cases

```
var_dump(
  router('/post/2'),
  router('/posts'),
  router('/post/5'),
  router('/comments/2'),
);
```

As was the case with the routes table, the results of the calls depicted above, each an evaluable route, can also be summarized in a table like Table 7.2.

7.4 Property Testing

Testing code is a great way to make assertions about its overall quality and conformance to the requirements that inform its behavior. In PHP, but really in many programming languages, writing tests is a standardized barometer by which to assess the compliance of programs with well-defined behavioral stipulations. Unit tests, in particular, are quite commonplace in most test suites as they are definitively granular. As far as Functional Programming is concerned, a unit is synonymous with a function—an assertion that makes sense given the imperative of the paradigm is to use functions as rules for manipulating (mostly) immutable states. Because pure functions have a black-box quality to them and behave in such a way as to conform to the type signatures that inform their design, the assertions made about them should factor in vast entropies to validate the type signatures and thus the strict behavioral properties they are bound by. Enter property tests, enhancements of unit tests whose emphasis is on rigorously checking, with vast prototypical input sets, that the rules that pure functions encode hold.

Popularized by the Haskell testing library QuickCheck, property testing is a technique for writing assertions about programs that enforces entropic rigor in evaluating testable units via fuzzing. Whenever fuzzing is deployed in testing code, it is used as a means of passing large batches of pseudorandom inputs to routines whose behavior is subject to inspection, ensuring that defects that would otherwise be overlooked are identified and removed. Pure functions are a great fit for inspection via property tests because their largely unambiguous nature lends itself to the creation of expressions that encode their behavior that can be summarized in the mantric expression "given x inputs, check whether y outputs of a certain variety are produced."

Demonstrating the viability of property testing can be done with a simple evaluation of the behavior of the mapr function written earlier in this chapter. `mapr`, to jog your memory, is a recursive higher-order function that applies an arbitrary function to all values in a numerically indexed array. Its type signature, written as follows, forms the blueprint for the testing to be performed with utilities in the eris library.

$$mapr :: (a \rightarrow b) \rightarrow [a] \rightarrow [b] \rightarrow Int \rightarrow [b] \qquad (7.4)$$

> Installing eris

Created and maintained by Giorgio Sironi, eris is the eminent property testing library in PHP. It is a port of the aforementioned QuickCheck that ships with a fuzzing tool built entirely atop memory-efficient generators. eris is interoperable with most testing libraries in PHP and should be installed to operationalize the test assertions written in this part of the text. To install eris, please type the following in a console of your choosing.

Installing eris via Composer

```
composer require --dev giorgiosironi/eris
```

The signature above dictates that given a function that transforms a value of type a to a value of type b, an array containing entries of type a, another array containing entries of type b, and an integer, the function `mapr` must return an array whose constituents are of type b. Per this notation, a and b are stand-ins for any kind of data, like the generic identifiers in the previous segment on pattern matching. Because the arguments $[b]$ and Int, which, respectively, are proxies for the accumulator and count necessary for the creation of a base case and non-cyclical sub-cases for recursion, are not necessarily required in validating the map operation, which in its idiomatic form does not expose them anyway, they can be ignored altogether. A leaner signature, that of the canonical map operation, should therefore inform the assertions to be performed. It can be expressed like so.

$$mapr :: (a \rightarrow b) \rightarrow [a] \rightarrow [b] \qquad (7.5)$$

With a type signature now defined, it is possible to write a simple property test for mapr with a combination of the assertion functions in the PHPUnit library and fuzzing tools in the eris suite. The assertions written in the snippet to follow converge the outputs of multiple generators of various types into an array and test the validity of mapr (or map) by checking whether it returns an array whose elements are of the type returned upon successful application of an arbitrary function to elements of the aforedescribed input list.

Property Testing with eris and PHPUnit

```
use Eris\{
  Generator,
  TestTrait,
};
use PHPUnit\Framework\TestCase;

class MaprTest extends TestCase
{
  use TestTrait;

  public function testmaprAppliesAFunctionToAllValuesInAnInput
  List(): void
  {
    $this
      ->forAll(
        Generator\int(),
        Generator\float(),
        Generator\bool(),
        Generator\string(),
        Generator\seq(
          Generator\nat(),
        ),
        Generator\constant(
          new stdClass(),
        ),
      )
      ->then(
        function (mixed ...$args): void {
          $result = mapr(\is_string(...), $args);

          $this->assertIsArray($result);
          $this->assertContainsOnlyBool($result);
        },
      );
  }
}
```

The test entropy for the test performed above includes integers, floating-point numbers, boolean values, strings, arrays, and an object. Though not exhaustive,

it suffices for the purpose of checking whether the type signature of `mapr` holds
for a multitude of prototypical inputs and is conclusively valid in its entirety (sort
of). The lambda chosen for the demonstration is the PHP-native is_string function,
whose purpose is to test whether a given input is of the string type. Its signature
is_string :: *a* → *Bool* stipulates that the function transforms its sole input into
a boolean value: a black-box evaluation congruent with its purpose. When applied
via mapr to the elements of the aforedescribed input list, `is_string` produces an
array made up entirely of boolean values. The two assertions in the example test
whether mapr produces an array and whether its composition reflects the result of
applying `is_string` indiscriminately to each entry in the input list. Types *a* and *b*
from the signature under investigation, per this test, are, respectively, polymorphic
and a proxy for boolean data. Running the assertions depicted via console directive
should produce a result that mirrors the following.

Running the Property Tests in a Console

```
$ vendor/bin/phpunit --bootstrap "vendor/autoload.php"
MaprTest.php
PHPUnit x.x.x by Sebastian Bergmann and contributors.

Runtime:        PHP x.x.x


.                                                    1 / 1 (100%)


Time: 00:00.029, Memory: 16.00 MB

OK (1 test, 200 assertions)
```

Because property tests condition the use of multiple data, they can be viewed
as a means of "stress testing" the validity of verifiable claims. Depending on the
nature of the properties under investigation, property testing can push the limits
of conciseness because testing with multiple forms of prototypical data increases
the likelihood of repetition and, thus, redundancy. Great care should be taken in
ensuring that non-duplicative testing efforts are avoided.

Consider this chapter complete at this point in the text. The assumption is that
you, the reader, are now equipped to embark on a quick tutorial in which concepts
interspersed throughout the book, in this chapter and the preceding ones, are pieced
together to create a simple program in an idiomatic Functional Programming style.
Please proceed to the next chapter with the same keenness shown in getting through
most of the instructional material presented up to this point.

Chapter 8
A Simple Project

8.1   Overview

This chapter aims to demonstrate how to build a simple phonebook, in the style of a shell/REPL, by composing functions. REPL, short for Read–Evaluate–Print–Loop, is simply a text-based interface that runs in perpetuity, producing a text output for every text input entered into it, per the rules of the evaluatory logic built into it. Such an interactive interface can be crafted with a few tools: the Functional Programming library used throughout most of the text, a console tabulation utility, and PHP streams. Before delving into the PHP representations of encodable phonebook elements, it is prudent to first stipulate the program's behavior and set targets for what to achieve. The following should prove adequate:

1. The phonebook should consist of a REPL and a registry. The former serves as the primary interface for manipulating records stored in the latter component.
2. The phonebook registry, a database of sorts, in which all phonebook records—names and phone numbers—are stored as key–value pairs, should exist as a single JSON file.
3. The registry-interactive actions supported by the REPL should include adding a contact, deleting a contact, and searching for a contact that matches a specified name input.

With the phonebook all "specced out," it is possible to proceed to define a directory structure for the application that is consistent with the specification laid out. The file topology relevant to the application can be summarized as follows.

M. B. Lochemem, *Functional Programming in PHP*,
https://doi.org/10.1007/979-8-8688-2468-5_8

File Topology for the Phonebook

```
- phonebook
  - src
    - registry
      - templates
        - interact.php
        - modify.php
      - add.php
      - constants.php
      - delete.php
      - search.php
    - repl
      - commands.php
      - constants.php
      - getline.php
      - putstr.php
  - vendor
  - registry.json
  - composer.json
  - composer.lock
  - phonebook
```

According to the structure above, the entry point of the application is the file phonebook, which is also the executable file to run in a console, to start the REPL. Its immediate dependencies reside in the folder named src and are categorically either registry-related, and thus residents of the registry subdirectory, or REPL-related and constituents of the subdirectory named repl. In each of these dependency folders are files that, respectively, house artifacts—functions and constants—that define the specific read- and write-related actions that can be performed directly on the registry file named registry.json and evaluatory input-related mechanisms for the REPL with which to effect reads and writes: the language that facilitates user interaction with the registry. Now that the targets have been set, it is possible to configure the application with Composer.

8.2   Wiring Things Up

With the specification laid out, wiring dependencies with Composer is now a clearer proposition. This wiring simply entails specifying third-party dependencies and configuring an autoloader required to render a composite inclusive of the said vendor packages and the dependencies yet to be written (those in the aforediscussed file topology) accessible via a single file, in a single entry point. Composer is such a handy tool in this regard, as it not only provides a way to download packages listed on Packagist, but also simultaneously obviates the need to write an autoloader from scratch and simplifies the process of effectively autoloading functions. To begin the process of wiring the disparate parts of the phonebook with Composer is the action of placing the following data inside the composer.json file in the project's root directory.

composer.json File for the Phonebook Project

```
{
  "require": {
    "chemem/bingo-functional": "^2",
    "mmarica/display-table": "^1",
    "ext-parallel": "*"
  },
  "autoload": {
    "psr-4": {
      "Phonebook\\": "src/"
    },
    "files": [
      "src/registry/templates/interact.php",
      "src/registry/templates/modify.php",
      "src/registry/add.php",
      "src/registry/constants.php",
      "src/registry/delete.php",
      "src/registry/search.php",
      "src/repl/commands.php",
      "src/repl/constants.php",
      "src/repl/getline.php",
      "src/repl/putstr.php"
    ]
  }
}
```

The project's vendor dependencies downloadable via console prompt, mentioned in the "Overview" section, are defined in the "require" section of the composer.json file. Included in this list is the Functional Programming library, bingo-functional, a tool with which to convert arrays to text tables in display-table, and the extension parallel introduced in Chapter 6, without which any console prompt will not run. Its immediate dependencies, namespaced under "Phonebook", are bootstrapped in the "files" section of the file. Defined in the section "files" is a list of paths to each registry- and REPL-categorized file in the project's file topology, paths that are ultimately registered in the autoloader generated by Composer upon the successful installation of all relevant vendor libraries.

To download all the dependencies required for the project and generate an autoloader to wire all dependencies, type the following in a console of your choosing. Ensure that the directive below is typed in an instance of a console, the present working directory of which is set to the project root.

Installing Project Dependencies with Composer

```
composer update
```

8.3 Writing Registry Functions

Because the registry is the most indispensable part of the phonebook, as without
it, no phonebook data can be created or retrieved, it makes sense to kick off the
coding exercise in this part of the book by building the scaffolding necessary for
interacting with the phonebook's de facto database. A good start would involve
defining a path to the registry as a constant. Since the registry placement in the
file topology is not likely to change and computing the path to the said file each
time it is needed for either a read or write operation would constitute duplicative
effort, this course of action is vindicated. Place the following definition in the file
"src/registry/constants.php".

Essential Registry Constants

```
namespace Phonebook\Registry;

use function Chemem\Bingo\Functional\filePath;

\define(
  __NAMESPACE__ . '\\PHONEBOOK_PATH',
  filePath(0, 'registry.json'),
);
```

Tandem use of PHP's `define` syntax that is more expressionally permissive than
`const` and the `filePath` function above ensures that the value assigned to the
constant "Phonebook \Registry \PHONEBOOK _PATH"is the absolute path to the
registry. After defining the registry path, sights can be set on defining the first of two
templates for interacting with the registry. Namespaced under "Phonebook \Registry
\Templates", the function named `interact` makes it possible to either read from the
registry or write to it in a CSP-compliant way. It conditionally bootstraps read and
write traces that can be expressed as follows.

$$seq\ ReadRegistry = \langle fread, jsondecode\rangle \tag{8.1}$$

$$seq\ WriteRegistry = \langle jsonencode, fwrite\rangle \tag{8.2}$$

The events *fread* and *jsondecode* are proxies for a file read and a lossless JSON-to-hashtable conversion first defined in Chapter 6, while events *jsonencode* and *fwrite* are representative of a hashtable-to-JSON conversion and a file write operation. Writing interact as a function capable of spawning both traces via runtime eliminates the duplicative effort of writing the same ext-parallel scaffolding twice, but more specifically, using a CSP standard, and therefore threads, parallelizes operations that are known to incur CPU blocking penalties in file reads and writes. The function `interact` looks like this.

Interact Function

```
namespace Phonebook\Registry\Templates;

use Chemem\Bingo\Functional\Functors\Monads\IO;
use parallel\{
  Channel,
  Runtime,
};

use function Chemem\Bingo\Functional\Functors\Monads\IO\IO;

use const Phonebook\Registry\PHONEBOOK_PATH;

function interact(Channel $channel, ?array $contents = null): IO
{
  return IO(
    function () use ($channel, $contents): mixed {
      $runtime = new Runtime();

      $runtime->run(
        ...(
          !$contents ?
            [
              function (string $file, Channel $channel): void {
                $channel->send(
                  @\json_decode(
                    \file_get_contents($file),
                    true,
                  ) ?? [],
                );
              },
              [PHONEBOOK_PATH, $channel],
            ] :
            [
              function (
                string $file,
                array $contents,
                Channel $channel,
              ): void {
                $channel->send(
                  \file_put_contents(
```

```
                    $file,
                    \json_encode($contents),
                  ),
                );
              },
              [
                PHONEBOOK_PATH,
                $contents,
                $channel,
              ],
            ]
          ),
        );

      return $channel->recv();
    },
  );
}
```

A call to `interact` with only a channel object bootstraps the trace
seq ReadRegistry, while invoking the same function with a hashtable passed
to its second parameter initiates the trace *seq WriteRegistry* and, thus, a write
operation. Encasing the results of instances of both parallel computations in an I/O
monad, a staple of the rest of this tutorial, simply guarantees that any side effects
from the threading process are diffused into a monadic context and the truthy values
that would signify success are rendered available for monadic composition.

The second of two registry templates, the function named `modify`, is useful
insofar as it provides the foundation upon which to define the specific registry
actions described in the "Overview" section. It builds on top of the aforedescribed
`interact` and provides a template for defining actions that write back to the registry
or simply stop at reading its contents. It looks like this.

Modify Function

```
namespace Phonebook\Registry\Templates;

use Chemem\Bingo\Functional\Functors\Monads\IO;
use parallel\Channel;

use function Chemem\Bingo\Functional\Functors\Monads\IO\IO;

function modify(
  Channel $channel,
  callable $action,
  bool $writeback = true,
): IO {
  return interact($channel)
    ->bind(
```

```
      fn (array $contents): IO =>
        IO(
          $action($contents),
        ),
    )
    ->bind(
      fn (array $contents): IO =>
        $writeback ?
          interact($channel, $contents) :
          IO($contents),
    );
}
```

The first call in a chain of monadic calls defined inside of `modify` is to read the contents of the registry via interact. Upon a successful read, the hashtable result sent via a channel is passed to the unary function passed as the second argument to the parent function and shuttled via the I/O monad to a function that, depending on whether a writeback is requested or not, either updates the registry with the modified contents or simply propagates them, again, via the I/O monad.

Now that the templates have been defined, it makes sense to proceed to create some actions. First on the list is **add**, a function in the category of "writeback" utilities that simply places a new item in the registry. It is written in such a way as to funnel the result of a lens set call into the template modify and takes on the following form.

Add Function

```
namespace Phonebook\Registry;

use Chemem\Bingo\Functional\Functors\Monads\IO;
use parallel\Channel;

use function Chemem\Bingo\Functional\Functors\Lens\{
  lensPath,
  set,
};
use function Phonebook\Registry\Templates\modify;

function add(
  Channel $channel,
  string $name,
  string $phone,
): IO {
  return modify(
    $channel,
    fn (array $contents): array =>
      set(
        lensPath($name),
```

```
            $phone,
            $contents,
        ),
    );
}
```

The lens in the signature of **add** simply assigns to its focal point set to the name of a contact by the function `lensKey` a corresponding phone number. The setter in `lensKey` internally calls the function `assocPath`, which creates an updated version of the list received upon a successful initial call to the function `interact`, appending to it a new contact–phone pair. In the ensuing write, the data in this updated list is persisted to the registry, and a new entry is created. Furthermore, because the setter, in creating such list updates, instantiates shallow list clones, amendments to phone numbers are registered as updates if slight changes are made to existing entries. **add** therefore works both as a creator of new entries and an updater of those that already exist in the registry.

Next is the function **delete** that purges a contact from the registry. Perhaps the most compact of the two writeback functions written thus far, **delete** simply implements an unset operation to purge a record identifiable by contact name from the list passed to the template modify. It looks like this.

Delete Function

```
namespace Phonebook\Registry;

use Chemem\Bingo\Functional\Functors\Monads\IO;
use parallel\Channel;

use function Phonebook\Registry\Templates\modify;

function delete(Channel $channel, string $name): IO
{
  return modify(
    $channel,
    function (array $contents) use ($name): array {
      unset($contents[$name]);

      return $contents;
    },
  );
}
```

To round up the slate of registry functions is **search**, the only non-writeback function. Internally, it filters out entries in the registry that do not match a specified search query. The filtration here is performed on contact names in a fold operation. The **search** function is as follows.

Search Function

```
namespace Phonebook\Registry;

use Chemem\Bingo\Functional\Functors\Monads\IO;
use parallel\Channel;

use function Chemem\Bingo\Functional\fold;
use function Phonebook\Registry\Templates\modify;

function search(Channel $channel, string $query): IO
{
  return modify(
    $channel,
    fn (array $contents): array =>
      fold(
        function (
          array $acc,
          string $phone,
          string $name,
        ) use ($query): array {
          if (
            (bool) \preg_match(
              \sprintf(
                '/(%s)/i',
                \preg_quote($query),
              ),
              $name,
            )
          ) {
            $acc[] = [$name, $phone];
          }

          return $acc;
        },
        $contents,
        [],
      ),
    false,
  );
}
```

In line with the running theme of removing duplicative effort, albeit with respect
to iteration here, the fold operation in the signature of search is geared toward
creating a new list of tuple*esque* pairs from contacts whose names match the input
provided in a search query. The iterative work otherwise performed in a sequence
defined by a call to filter and then a follow-up invocation of map is done in
a single iteration, with a single fold call. In this form, the function search not
only filters out non-matching contacts, but also creates a list of matching contacts

congruent with the ASCII table generation API used somewhere in the next slate of
utilities.

8.4   Writing REPL Functions

Onto the final slate of functions, the REPL-related ones. Generally, the utilities
defined in this section are those that directly shape the medium of interaction
between the user and the registry. In this set of REPL functions are tools with which
to mold everything regarding presentation, validation, and filesystem access. As was
the case with the registry utilities, the starting point here is the constants.php file in
the "src/repl" subdirectory. Again, like the registry, the REPL suite contains only
one constant, the character sequence to display each time a user is prompted to
provide parsable input, at the start of each input cycle. The text ">>>" provides
adequate instructive value and is deserving of a placement in the REPL slate as the
immutable value assigned to the constant REPL _PROMPT that will prove useful in
the final part of the walkthrough. Usage of the const keyword suffices here, unlike
before.

Essential REPL Prompt

```php
namespace Phonebook\Repl;

const REPL_PROMPT = '>>> ';
```

Up next is the first of two filesystem functions called `getline`, which reads
a line of text from the Standard Input Device (STDIN) and propagates it, also
(thematically) via an instance of the I/O monad. This function, depicted in the
next snippet, is responsible for operationalizing the "R" in REPL and imputes its
compactness to PHP's robust streams API.

getline Function

```php
namespace Phonebook\Repl;

use Chemem\Bingo\Functional\Functors\Monads\IO;

use function Chemem\Bingo\Functional\Functors\Monads\IO\IO;

function getline(): IO
{
  return IO(
    fn (): string =>
```

```
      \rtrim(
        \fgets(STDIN),
        "\r\n",
      ),
    );
  }
```

Also attributable to the same streams API is the conciseness of the function putstr, which effects the "P" in REPL. As its name suggests, putstr writes text (by default) to the Standard Output Device (STDOUT) and is quite behaviorally similar to a Haskell function of the same name. The variant defined here, however, offers more optionality to a caller in the form of a bigger arity, which can be seen in the snippet below.

putstr Function

```
namespace Phonebook\Repl;

use Chemem\Bingo\Functional\Functors\Monads\IO;

use function Chemem\Bingo\Functional\Functors\Monads\IO\IO;

function putstr(
  string $data,
  bool $linebreak = false,
  mixed $fd        = \STDOUT,
): IO {
  return IO(
    fn (): int|bool =>
      \fwrite(
        $fd,
        $linebreak ?
          \sprintf("%s%s", $data, \PHP_EOL) :
          $data,
      ),
  );
}
```

With the version of `putstr` defined above, it is possible to not only specify whether or not to add an OS-relevant linebreak to an output string, but also the file descriptor to which to write output data. A default call to putstr effects standard behavior that may not always work. In some cases like printing REPL output, a linebreak might be required. Such cases contrast scenarios like those in which a prompt is to be displayed on a screen at the start of each input cycle. Accounting for such scenarios by parameterizing serves to further demonstrate the parsimony in the Dao of reducing otherwise duplicative effort.

Table 8.1 Summary of REPL syntax

Pattern	Purpose
`["add", name, phone]`	Adding a new contact
`["search", name]`	Searching the registry for a contact
`["delete", name]`	Deleting a record from the registry
`["exit"]`	Terminating the REPL
`_`	Signifying invalid input

Last on this list of REPL functions is **commands** whose semantics mirror those of a rudimentary parser-combinator. The function **commands** defines the syntax of the REPL and with it, the evaluatory logic that characterizes step "E." Fit for purpose is pattern matching, introduced in the previous chapter, that can be adapted to implement the syntactic options summarized in Table 8.1.

It is clear from the tabular summary of functionality above that the function **commands** is the point at which registry and REPL functions converge. It is the part of the phonebook in which each syntactic pattern prescribed in the "Overview" section is matched with its registry-shaping action, much like controllers and request methods with resource-relevant endpoints, in web apps. The template for the function **commands** is as follows.

Commands Function

```
namespace Phonebook\Repl;

use Chemem\Bingo\Functional\Functors\Monads\IO;
use Mmarica\DisplayTable;
use parallel\Channel;

use function Chemem\Bingo\Functional\{
  PatternMatching\patternMatch as pmatch,
};
use function Phonebook\Registry\{
  add,
  delete,
  search,
};

function commands(Channel $channel, string $input): IO
{
  return pmatch(
    [
      // patterns go here...
    ],
    \preg_split('/(\s){1,}/', $input),
  );
}
```

The patterns to be slotted into Table 8.1 can be described one by one in order of appearance in the syntax list. First on the list, the pattern ["add", name, phone], describes addition syntax parsable by the REPL. To the binary function assigned to it in Table 8.1 are passed a name and phone number, the latter of which is subjected to a format check by way of regular expression. Numbers that do not feature anywhere between 9 and 14 digits after the plus (+) sign are flagged as invalid: an error message is written to the Standard Error Device (STDERR), and the next input cycle is started. Those that pass this test are stored in the registry. The syntax facilitative of adding a contact looks like this.

Add Command Template

```
'["add", name, phone]' => fn (string $name, string $phone): IO =>
  !(bool) \preg_match('/^(\+){1}(\d+){10,13}$/', $phone) ?
    putstr(
      \sprintf(
        'Number %s is invalid',
        $phone,
      ),
      true,
      \STDERR,
    ) :
    add(
      $channel,
      $name,
      $phone,
    )
      ->bind(
        fn (): IO =>
          putStr(
            \sprintf('%s added', $name),
            true,
          ),
      ),
```

Next is the search template ["search", name] to which a unary function is assigned. On a successful match, when a name-based search is attempted, the registry function of a similar name is invoked, and its result is passed to an ASCII table generator to output a table similar to that produced by a console interface like MariaDB's. Something like the following works.

Search Command Template

```
'["search", name]' => fn (string $name): IO =>
  search($channel, $name)
    ->bind(
```

```
      fn (array $contents): IO =>
        putStr(
          DisplayTable::create()
            ->headerRow(['Name', 'Phone number'])
            ->dataRows($contents)
            ->toText()
            ->generate(),
          true,
        ),
    ),
```

The delete template ["delete", name] is just as simple as the registry function
invoked in its assigned unary function scope. Once a deletion occurs, the message
"name deleted" is printed by the REPL. The following accounts for inputs like
"delete Seb."

Delete Command Template

```
'["delete", name]' => fn (string $name): IO =>
  delete($channel, $name)
    ->bind(
      fn (): IO =>
        putStr(
          \sprintf('%s deleted', $name),
          true,
        ),
    ),
```

The tersest of the refutable patterns in the list, ["exit"], is treated as a voluntary
termination of the REPL for which the response is a neat termination message and
graceful program exit. Such termination is accounted for in the following snippet.

Exit Command Template

```
'["exit"]' => fn (): IO =>
  putStr(
    'Thanks for using the phonebook',
    true,
  )
    ->map(
      fn (): mixed => \exit(),
    ),
```

Finally, the wildcard_that matches all inputs not accounted for in the table. As the only irrefutable pattern in the table, it serves as a handler for all data that cannot be parsed by the REPL and thus outputs a fitting message.

Irrefutable Wildcard Template

```
'_' => fn (): IO =>
  putStr(
    'Invalid command',
    true,
    \STDERR,
  ),
```

At this point, the REPL is almost complete. Parts R, E, and P are all but surely accounted for. All that is left is the L part, the loop behavior that renders the aforediscussed (R)eading, (E)valuatng, and (P)rinting repeatable.

8.5   Finishing the REPL

The looping required to render the work done thus far repeatable should occur at a point in the project where all the utilities required converge. This critical intersection point, per the structural blueprint defined earlier in the chapter, is the script eponymous with the application—phonebook. Inside of this script, the autoloader is invoked, the dedicated channel that powers the CSP-style threading used in the registry is defined, and the infinite loop into which the command function is woven is started. Finishing the REPL means writing this phonebook script and therefore fashioning it like so.

Phonebook Entry Point Script

```
#!/usr/bin/env php
require_once __DIR__ . '/vendor/autoload.php';

use Chemem\Bingo\Functional\Functors\Monads\IO;
use parallel\Channel;

use function Phonebook\Repl\{
  commands,
  getline,
  putstr,
};

use const Phonebook\Repl\REPL_PROMPT;
```

```
$channel = new Channel();

while (true) {
  putStr(REPL_PROMPT)
    ->bind(
      getLine(...),
    )
    ->bind(
      fn (string $command): IO => commands($channel, $command),
    )
    ->exec();
}

$channel->close();
```

That is it. The REPL is complete. To run it, type one of either ./phonebook
or php phonebook in a terminal of your choosing, in the root directory of the
phonebook project. You should see something like this when you open it (afresh) in
the console.

Firing Up the REPL

```
>>>
```

Try to create a new contact. Via the add command, attempt to add Michael's
phone number "+254795151763" to the registry. You should see something like
this.

Adding a Contact

```
>>> add Michael +254795151763
Michael added
```

Now try to search the phonebook for the contact you just added. Type the command "search michael" to search the phonebook for Michael's contact information.
You should get a result that appears as in the image below.

Searching for a Specific Contact

```
>>> search mic
.---------.---------------.
|  Name   | Phone number  |
:---------+---------------:
| Michael | +254795151763 |
'---------'---------------'
```

Add phone numbers for Sheridan, Alex, and Jeffrey: more imaginary contacts. Attempt to delete Alex's contact information. You should see, after successful deletion, a registry from which Alex's details are absent.

Another Keyword Search

```
>>> search e
.----------.---------------.
|   Name   | Phone number  |
:----------+---------------:
| Michael  | +254795151763 |
| Sheridan | +13478112199  |
| Jeffrey  | +256712243903 |
'----------'---------------'
```

Before terminating the REPL, try to enter something erroneous—perhaps something like a non-parsable print command to see if the parser's wildcard function works. The console should display a message that reads "Invalid command."

Print and Exit Commands

```
>>> print
Invalid command
>>> exit
Thanks for using the phonebook
```

That concludes the tutorial. The phonebook discussed in this chapter behaves like a prototypical shell and is constructed from ideas discussed throughout this book. It is, however, merely a window into crafting PHP apps in accordance with canonical Functional Programming principles. You are probably bound to write more complicated apps than the one shown in this chapter of the text, and it is my hope that you develop the consistency required to build applications from reusable functions in such a way as to not expend more effort than is needed.

Appendix

The contents of the list to follow are resources—texts and videos—that will likely prove useful in furthering an understanding of Functional Programming. The programming languages featured in some of the instructional materials in the entries that follow may not be PHP or its offshoot dialects; however, the universality of the fundamentals discussed throughout this book should render the snippets as well as the concepts they demonstrate understandable to a reader with a PHP background.

A.1   Functional PHP

Written by Gilles Crettenand, the creator of the Functional-PHP organization on GitHub, the book *Functional PHP* makes for an interesting read. Its contents are a nice supplement to the material offered in this book, as it has a similar structure and delves into the same ideas, as well as a few rather nuanced Functional Programming topics more suited to PHP developers looking to actualize in their entirety ideas more prevalent in purer functional syntaxes like Haskell and OCaml.

A.2   Composing Software

The brainchild of Eric Elliott of JavaScriptScene fame, *Composing Software*, is a distillation of Functional Programming ideas for JavaScript enthusiasts. Effectively the culmination of a series of blog posts centered on the topic of composing functions in creative ways, via the application of techniques like mixins, lenses, and transducers, the book is a comprehensive guide on how to make paradigmatic ideas work in JavaScript. It can provide inspiration for patterns implementable in both PHP and JavaScript, languages often used in conjunction with each other, and

© The Author(s), under exclusive license to APress Media, LLC,   157
part of Springer Nature 2026
M. B. Lochemem, *Functional Programming in PHP*,
https://doi.org/10.1007/979-8-8688-2468-5

therefore increase the potential for some truly interesting Functional Programming crossover.

A.3   Hoogle

There is currently no PHP equivalent to the type signature search engine, Hoogle, that is native to the Haskell ecosystem. What makes Hoogle particularly intriguing is that it provides a means of checking the validity of type signatures and can offer a window into writing entirely new or hyperintensional PHP variants of functions that exist in the Haskell userspace. The placement of Hoogle on this list is not an outright appeal to learn Haskell or any pure Functional Programming language, for that matter: it is a means of inspiring plumbing in PHP geared toward creating patterns like the aforediscussed lenses and functors.

A.4   Bartosz Milewski's Functional Programming Talks

Bartosz Milewski is one of the foremost experts on Functional Programming. Although he is not a PHP aficionado, Mr. Milewski, a C++ and Haskell devotee, gives many talks at various conferences about Category Theory and writes insightful articles on the same topic. Because the articles might seem a little dense with Functional Programming jargon, the talks, purposed for developers of different backgrounds, might be a little more interesting and easier to follow. You can find a playlist with a selection of Mr. Milewski's talks on YouTube.

Index

GPSR Compliance
The European Union's (EU) General Product Safety Regulation (GPSR) is a set
of rules that requires consumer products to be safe and our obligations to
ensure this.

If you have any concerns about our products, you can contact us on

ProductSafety@springernature.com

In case Publisher is established outside the EU, the EU authorized
representative is:

Springer Nature Customer Service Center GmbH
Europaplatz 3
69115 Heidelberg, Germany